THE STANHOPE & TYNE RAILROAD COMPANY

ROB LANGHAM

AMBERLEY

First published 2020

Amberley Publishing
The Hill, Stroud,
Gloucestershire, GL5 4EP

www.amberley-books.com

ISBN: 978 1 4456 9766 6 (print)
ISBN: 978 1 4456 9767 3 (ebook)

British Library Cataloguing in Publication Data.
A catalogue record for this book is available from the British Library.

Typeset in 10pt on 13pt Celeste.
Origination by Amberley Publishing.
Printed in the UK.

Contents

Introduction

The Stanhope & Tyne Railroad Company (S&TR) had a remarkable but brief existence. It still seems incredible that its route, and the varied methods of moving the wagons of lime, limestone and coal along it, ever existed. Although at the time of its opening railways, known as waggonways, had operated in the North East of England for centuries, the scale of the S&TR's operations was unmatched. Apart from the Stockton & Darlington Railway of 1825, it was the only railway company of any size in the North East when it opened. The Stanhope & Tyne is also well known for its financial failure and its near ruining of famous railway engineer Robert Stephenson. The history in-between the beginning and end of the railway company is little covered, partly owing to lack of evidence for it – the company records that do survive are mostly sales ledgers that offer little by way of actual history, although the locomotive working records are of interest. Much of the history that follows comes from those writing about railways at the period – or those in the years after using what documents or personal accounts they had available (which do not appear to survive now) – and from newspaper accounts which, as today, particularly focus on bad news. Accidents and incidents are a common theme in early railway history and the S&TR is no exception.

Following the downfall of the S&TR, the route proved to be profitable through their movement of lime, limestone and coal, as originally intended. The last years of steam on the line are particularly well remembered for the hard-working locomotives hauling trains of iron ore up to Consett Steel Works, and have been well covered in magazines and books since. This book attempts to tell more about this early railway than has been done before, and, together with the carefully chosen images, hopefully convey something of the atmosphere of the line and its varied, fascinating history. The main focus of this book is on the original Stanhope & Tyne Railroad and its immediate successors. A more detailed account of the Stockton & Darlington Railway's operation of half on the line under the name of the Wear & Derwent Railway is planned to follow.

CHAPTER 1

Origins

William Wallis of Westoe, near South Shields, signed a lease in 1831 for Pontop Colliery, including the right to mine for coal around Medomsley. That same year he signed a further lease to mine at West Consett. The following month he started a partnership with Cuthbert Rippon of Stanhope and William Harrison of Monkwearmouth Grange to quarry limestone (for building material, agricultural use and – increasingly – for the production of iron and steel) at Stanhope, and mine for coal around Medomsley. While these locations were rich in these minerals, they were far inland, away from the waterways that were vital in moving the minerals to the point of sale if they were to be sold in large quantities, rather than limited sales in the local area. Road transport at the time was inadequate for the movement of large quantities of minerals, with waggonways being used to transport minerals (usually coal) in the North East since the 1600s. Predating the use of steam locomotives on iron rails by around two hundred years, waggonways used horses that pulled wagons on wooden rails to a location on a river or the coast where they could be sent onward by water transport.

Fortunately, Harrison already had experience in waggonways. The obvious route would be to run a waggonway from Stanhope to Consett (near to Medomsley), then along the Derwent Valley to the River Tyne. This itself would have been a lengthy line for the time and would have to pass the difficult high ground between Stanhope and Consett; it was, however, not insurmountable. The main drawback with this was that the ships needed to take the minerals to markets such as London were not able to get as far upstream as Derwenthaugh, where the Derwent joined the Tyne. For the waggonways using these upper parts of the Tyne, the method was to load the coal into a keelboat (a wide, shallow vessel holding just over 20 tonnes of coal) at staiths or spouts. These would sail, row or ride the tide downriver to waiting ships, which would have to be loaded from the keelboat by shovel. Not only was this a time-consuming and labour-intensive process, with the added costs arising from this, but it increased breakages, and larger coal commanded a higher price at market.

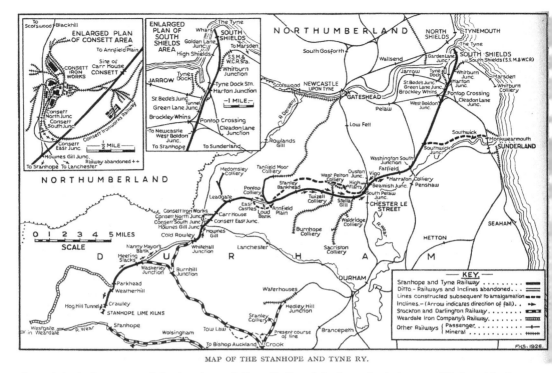

MAP OF THE STANHOPE AND TYNE RY.

The original 1834 route of the Stanhope & Tyne Railroad, its later deviations and links with the local railway network as of 1926.

Instead the decision was made to build a railway all the way from Stanhope to near the Tyne's mouth, at South Shields, where the mineral traffic could be directly loaded into the ships. This was a tremendous undertaking, but thanks to recent developments in railways, including the use of steam power for stationary engines working rope-hauled inclines, steam locomotives that had been in use in the North East since the 1810s, and the introduction and improvement of iron rails, it was not an impossible one – although very expensive. This line, the first major railway to be built in the North East since the Stockton & Darlington Railway, would be almost 34 miles long on the main route, excluding branches. In many ways similar to its more famous forebearer, in that they both were to use a mixture of locomotives, inclined planes and horse-worked sections, as well as being primarily occupied in the movement of minerals, unlike the Stockton & Darlington Railway, which used an Act of Parliament to acquire the land needed and the rights to run trains on it, this railway would use wayleaves. Wayleaves were common for waggonways – which effectively this railway was just a longer, more advanced version of – where the land was rented from the landowners for an agreed price. This saved the hassle of going through Parliament where objections could be made but could come at a high price. It was also felt that by using wayleaves the railway could hide its objective of running a lengthy railway and acquiring further rights for mining along the route of the line from any potential objectors.

Starting at the Stanhope end of the line, the Bishop of Durham owned the land over the high moors the line would have to cross, and talks started in December 1831 to gain the rights to lay a railway on this land. The scene was set, but railways were not cheap and so the Stanhope & Tyne Railroad Company was formed with a capital of £150,000 and started looking for investors. Plenty were found, mainly in London, and the first board of directors met in London in June 1832. Others joined the company, and although Cuthbert and Rippon decided continue, a lease was signed with Rippon for the quarries at Stanhope, and with a Charles Smythe for the lease of Pontop Colliery. The wealth backing the S&TR meant the work was to be done at the highest quality, with the two engineers for the line – consulting engineer Robert Stephenson and resident engineer Thomas Elliott (T. E.) Harrison (son of William Harrison), two of the finest in the land – having recently worked on the London & Birmingham Railway. As engineer of the railway, T. E. Harrison was responsible for its operations, his office being located at the railway's headquarters in South Shields. For Robert Stephenson, the railway was just another one of his works before moving on to something else (and being one of many customers for his engine manufactory) – until 1841 when the downfall of the company nearly ruined him.

CHAPTER 2

Building the Line

Construction started in July 1832, at the Stanhope end of the line, commencing from the limestone quarries and the company's limekilns at Crawleyside, to the north of Stanhope itself. For the part of the line from Crawleyside, and over the Waskerley moors, the line was roughly laid on the moors so, aside from Hog Hill Tunnel, which began shortly after the line commenced from the limekilns, it required little in terms of groundworks. By October a further section of line between Healeyfield and Hownes was commenced and orders were made for fish-bellied iron rails (weighing either 30 or 40 lbs per yard) and iron rail chairs, which would sit on stone blocks. Construction started on four stone engine houses for the stationary steam engines, which would work the inclines required to haul wagons over steep gradients. The famous mining engineer John Buddle was hired for his advice and work to reopen the collieries owned by the company started.

Opposite and this page: The S&TR limekilns at Crawleyside. It has been suggested in the past that the larger kilns were the work of the Stockton & Darlington Railway, but they appear to have already been in place when the Stockton & Darlington Railway took over in 1845. (Beamish Museum)

As construction proceeded eastward, the true purpose of the line was becoming clear to those not involved in the railway. Whereas the Bishop and Dean & Chapter of Durham had charged normal rates for wayleaves for the line between Stanhope and Medomsley, higher charges were asked for, and received – after all, there was little choice – the closer to South Shields the line got. This was also the case with other landowners, which included the Earl of Durham. To the east of Annfield, it was hoped to purchase the Beamish waggonway, which ran from the colliery at Beamish towards the Wear, for part of the route, which itself had been recently relaid with iron rails, but an agreement could not be made so a separate railway was built from West Stanley to Stella Gill.

The railway was to use the finest machinery available – the most up-to-date locomotives in the land for moving mineral traffic were ordered from Robert Stephenson & Co., as well as two of the stationary engines for inclines. The rate of construction of the line showed a desire to get the line built and open as soon as possible so the investors could get a return on their money. This also appears to be the case with the steam engines – the orders for the stationary steam engines were made with a variety of suppliers, no more than two per supplier, likely to ensure swift delivery.

At the eastern end of the line, at South Shields, construction started in the spring of 1833. Originally, it was hoped for the line to run through the town on the level. However, the Improvement Commission there demanded it be built higher so that it crossed King Street at no less than 15 feet above the roadway by way of 'gears' (a wooden bridge). Just before

In 2019 the route of the S&TR still runs high through South Shields. Here it crosses King Street, the wooden bridge long replaced and, until recently, the site of the Metro light rail station, which is now located to the south.

reaching King Street, the line, which from West Boldon had been on a northerly course, swung towards the west – that is, away from the sea – to the site of the drops on the River Tyne at Long Row. There was a public landing there that was taken over by the railway for the construction of the drops, and in return the company paid for Richardsons Quay and the street east of it to be widened, and Broad Landing was constructed/extended.[1] The bridge over King Street was erected on 20 November 1833 and the S&TR was described as 'proceeding rapidly in the formation of their line of way'.[2]

The coming railway was used to advertise local sales of property. The sellers, in March 1834, of a large estate near Stanhope, which included a quarry and mines, keenly included the fact it was 2.5 miles from the line of the railway, going on to extol the virtues of the property:

> To persons possessed of Capital, this Investment holds out Inducements rarely to be met with; the Stanhope and Tyne Railway will be completed in a short Time, and Markets thereby opened for the ready Disposal of the Produce of the Mines and Quarries.[3]

The total length of the line came to 37.75 miles. The main line of the railway was 33 miles, seven furlongs and one chain long, added to which there were originally three branches. The Medomsley branch was 1 mile, three furlongs and five chains, Tanfield Moor branch 2 miles and one furlong, and the Stuart Pit branch two furlongs.

Hog Hill Tunnel, built in 1833 at the foot of the Crawleyside incline near the start of the S&TR.

1 Hodgson, G. B., *The Borough of South Shields: From the Earliest Period to the Close of the Nineteenth Century* (Newcastle: Andrew Reid & Co., 1903), p. 384
2 *Newcastle Courant*, 23 November 1833
3 *Newcastle Courant*, 29 March 1834

The route and workings of the line itself are necessary to give an idea of the complex and diverse working nature of this incredible railway. Starting at the limekilns at Crawleyside, Stanhope, 796 feet above sea level, the start of the journey for the wagons loaded with either lime or limestone was up the 0.5-mile-long Crawleyside incline with gradients of 1 in 12 and 1 in 8 and included the short Hog Hill Tunnel. Crawleyside was worked by a 50 hp steam engine. The top of inclines were known as the 'head' with the bottom known as the 'foot'. Inclines were also known as 'Planes' or 'Banks'. Men known as bankriders would ride the wagons to operate the brake, a dangerous occupation that remained throughout the use of the inclines. At Crawleyside incline head, the rope used for hauling the wagons up was thrown off and a new one attached to pull them up the Weatherhill incline, which began immediately, just over a mile in length with gradients of 1 in 21 and 1 in 13. The engine at Weatherhill was again a 50 hp steam engine and, like the Crawleyside engine, built by Hawks of Gateshead. The engine at Crawleyside could haul two or three wagons at a time, and the engine at Weatherhill four or six, owing to the easier overall gradient.

Weatherhill incline was one of the best-known parts of the railway, remaining so owing to the survival of the original engine at the National Railway Museum, York. The tall, impressive engine house stood, long after it was replaced in 1919, until it became dangerous and was demolished in the 1960s. The following description and sketch of the 1833 Weatherhill engine was printed in 1919 following its replacement:

The single cylinder of the engine is 2 ft 5 inches in diameter and has a 5 ft stroke. The piston is worked through a parallel motion composed of two large swinging arms, or beams, with intermediate links. These arms, as will be seen from the sketch, are anchored to brackets in the outer walls. An examination of the sketch will enable even those entirely without engineering knowledge to understand how the vertical motion given to the piston rod is communicated through pinion gear to the drums. On the crank shaft, which is 18 ft 6 inches above the floor level, is fixed a pinion working in gear with the large spur wheel on each drum, and on this shaft just behind the crank is the eccentric for working the slide valve in the steam chest on the side of the cylinder.

The eccentric sheave is loose on the shaft and the reversal of the engine is accomplished, as is usual in these old single-cylinder engines, by means of a 'gab' (hook) end to the eccentric rod. To reverse the engine the 'gab' has to be removed from the pin on end of weigh bar working valve gear by means of a lever under the control of the engine man. This allows the eccentric to drop. The valve is then put into corresponding position by lever (also under control of engineman) and the gab pushed on by foot levers and the engine restarted will run in opposite direction, the engine crank taking hold of the eccentric sheave by a projecting catch which meets a similar catch on the sheave. All this, of course, meant heavy work for the engineman, with a very careful handling of the steam regulator valve.

Fortunately for those not able to visualise the workings of the machine by the description and sketches, in 1924 the engine was removed from its house and put on display in the railway museum at Queen Street, York. In order to fit, the original flywheel was cut in half and, on relocation to the current Leeman Road site, a replica full-size flywheel was made.

Above and below: Crawleyside incline engine house. It is not known if the building changed substantially after the change of engine to a marine type in the 1880s. (Beamish Museum)

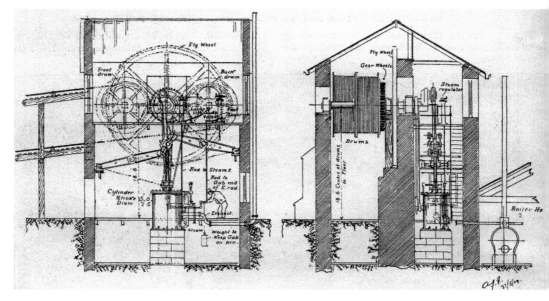

Left side and front diagram showing the workings of the original 1833 Weatherhill incline engine made in 1919.

Some other moving parts have also been changed, and the original cylinder was replaced later in the nineteenth century. Despite this, it remains a highly impressive remnant of the S&TR. On most days the engine is demonstrated by electric motor where it can be marvelled at in motion.

The summit at Weatherhill – also known as Whiteleahead – was later known as the highest point on the English railway system at 1,445 feet above sea level, only beaten in Britain by Dalnaspidal summit on the Highland Railway (although a few private railways were higher – the Snowdon Mountain Railway an obvious example. The nearby Weatherhill & Rookhope Railway reached 1,600 feet). For 1.5 miles on top of the moors, a bleak, harsh environment, the wagons were pulled by horses. At Parkhead (to the north of the later station site), a wheelhouse provided a tail rope that lowered the wagons down to Meeting Slacks engine house, which powered the rope. The tail rope worked by being attached to the rear of the wagons, lowering them downhill safely at a controlled speed rather than directly pulling them towards the engine house. Another rope was attached at Meeting Slacks to lower the wagons further down the line.

From a place later known as Waskerley, which under the Stockton & Darlington Railway became a significant railway community, the Meeting Slacks incline ended. A self-acting incline then followed, which earned the unusual name of Nanny Mayers incline. Nanny Mayer, who lived with her family in a house just 200 yards from the incline, around halfway down its length, sold ale to the railway workers and turned her home into a tavern. From the bottom of Nanny Mayers incline for the next 3.25 miles through Whiteleahead and Cold Rowley, the section was worked by horses, although for the last 2 miles the horses actually rode in dandy carts at the rear of the wagons (a wagon the horse would climb onto where the gradient allowed the wagons to roll downhill by gravity – supposedly

The Weatherhill engine on display at the National Railway Museum, York.

The site of Meeting Slacks incline engine house. The line continued to the right of the image to the site of Waskerley, where the line descended down Nanny Mayer's incline.

Cutting near the head of Nanny Mayer's incline, looking down the incline.

The remains of the Railway Inn, home of Nanny Mayer.

the invention of George Stephenson and introduced first on the Stockton & Darlington Railway) towards the daunting prospect of Hownes Gill, a ravine that is 160 feet deep and 800 feet wide at the top.

A bridge across the gill was the obvious option but would be highly expensive and was further complicated by the poor ground conditions at the bottom of the gill. Robert Stephenson came up with an unusual solution: stationary engine-worked inclines. A single stationary engine was placed at the bottom of Hownes Gill on a rectangular platform, working the two inclines on each side of the ravine. One of the inclines had a gradient of 1 in 2 1/2, the other 1 in 3. The stationary engine worked one wagon down at a time sideways on a cradle, and when reaching the base of the incline was moved to another cradle, where it was again placed sideways until it reached the top of the ravine. This required multiple small turntables to place the wagons sideways, then straight again at the base of the incline, then sideways again, etc., and was both very labour intensive and slow. Hownes Gill incline would remain a severe bottleneck for the movement of wagons along the line for over twenty years.

After traversing Hownes Gill, the wagons were attached to the rope from the Carr House engine, which pulled them up a 1 in 71 gradient for 1.25 miles then let them down the other side on a 1 in 108 gradient for 0.75 miles. The short branch here to Consett

Healeyfield Bridge, near Rowley, on the original part of the horse-worked line between the foot of Nanny Mayer's incline and Hownes Gill incline.

Hownes Gill viaduct under construction *c.* 1858. This fascinating oblique photo gives a unique view of the original S&TR engine house and details of the incline and the central platform arrangement. (Head of Steam – Darlington Railway Museum)

Pit was the first coal mine on the line, 11 miles from the start of the line. That entire 11 miles, built at great expense and with five stationary engines on its route, was solely for the movement of limestone and lime from the kilns at Crawleyside, and there was no significant traffic that could be gained en route. From this point onwards, though, the north-west Durham coalfield, and all its riches, was now accessible. It was the movement of this down to the Tyne that would be the major source of income for the route for over 100 years. Another branch led to the pit at Medomsley, owned by the S&TR. The next 2.25 miles from the east foot of Carr House incline were worked by horses to a point known as Bantling Castle, believed to be after the 'Bantams', the miners of short stature who lived here.

A ridge near Pontop Pike had to be travelled over, and this was done by a stationary engine at the top of Loud Bank. The west side of the incline was 662 yards and the engine then lowered the wagons down 1,056 yards to Annfield. Annfield soon became known as Annfield Plane, and later Annfield Plain, owing to the inclined plane. From here there was another horse-worked section of over 2.5 miles, known as the Stanley Level. Another branch led the 2 miles to Tanfield Moor Colliery, which previously had sent its coals down the Tanfield Waggonway, which had been in operation for over a century before. Stanley is on the edge of a high plateau, which looks over the rest of County Durham to its east. From Stanley there were four self-acting inclines in a row – Stanley, Twizell, Eden Hill and Waldridge, as well as the Pelton Level, which was worked by horses for almost a mile. At the end of the Pelton Level, when Pelton Fell was reached, there was a branch heading south serving Pelton and Waldridge collieries. At Pelton Fell was an area known as Stella Gill, which became a huge marshalling yard for the coal wagons that transited through the area. A stationary engine to the east at High Flatts worked the Stella Gill level of three quarters of a mile by tail rope, and then let the wagons descend the other side of the engine towards the turnpike road to Durham, which had a level crossing. The turnpike road was also known as the Great North Road, later known as the A1 and now the A167. There was then a final set of two inclines worked by a double engine at Vigo, which pulled the wagons up towards itself from the turnpike road and then down the other side to Fatfield Gears, a bridge over the Biddick Burn – a distance of almost 2 miles.

From Biddick Burn to South Shields the line was worked by locomotive, the gradients here being nigh on non-existent compared to the journey the wagons had taken already. From Biddick Burn the railway swept on a north-east heading towards Boldon, then north up towards South Shields. Owing to the lack of major gradients, the final 9 miles operated by locomotives had little in the way of engineering works, apart from the bridges at South Shields mentioned previously. Taken as a whole, the route, the country crossed by it, and the methods employed in operating the railway were nothing short of incredible. There were nine stationary incline engines, some of them working two inclines at a time, five self-acting inclines comprising 3 miles of the route, and horses originally working 10.5 miles of the main line of the railway, as well as the branches. To work the locomotive section, orders were placed with Robert Stephenson & Co. The afternoon of Thursday 8 May 1834 saw the first locomotive placed on the rails at

British Railways days view of Q6 Class locomotive 63366 heading towards Consett at Bantling Castle. In the background Loud Bank can be seen. Until 1886 it was worked by an incline adjacent to the left of the visible road with a stationary engine at the top of the hill, all long gone by the time this photograph was taken. (Beamish Museum)

Photo taken from near the same position (on the opposite side of the bridge) in 2019, still clearly showing the road adjacent to the Loud Bank incline. The 1835 S&TR limekilns are visible to the right centre.

Stanley incline head in the early twentieth century, showing four North Eastern Railway P7 20-tonne hoppers. Apart from the development of coal wagons and improvements in track, the self-working gravity inclines, whereby the weight of descending loaded wagons pulled up, via a rope going round the wheel at the head of the incline, empty wagons, on the S&TR likely changed very little in their appearance and operation over the years. (Head of Steam – Darlington Railway Museum)

Waldridge incline Bank Foot. (Beamish Museum)

Waldridge incline Bank Head in December 1938. (Beamish Museum)

Biddick level crossing and signalbox looking east in May 1982 after the closure of the line. This is approximately the point on the line where on the S&TR locomotives would take over from the foot of the final incline on the line towards South Shields. (Beamish Museum)

South Shields.[4] The western section of the line, from Crawleyside to Annfield, was, by this point, nearly ready to be opened and, as was customary for railways at the time, this was a cause for celebration, the official opening of this half of the line taking place on 15 May 1834:

A party of gentlemen left Annfield at eight o'clock in the morning, by a railway wagon tastefully fitted up for the occasion, and arrived at the termination of the line about eleven, highly gratified with the whole line of road, but especially with that part of it which crosses the precipitous ravine called the Hownes. At one o'clock, the first four lime carriages were started from the spacious range of kilns belonging to the Company, and speedily ascended the steep inclined plane adjoining Stanhope, amidst the cheers of an immense crowd of spectators, who, notwithstanding the wetness of the early part of the morning, had assembled from all parts of the adjacent country. A splendid dinner had been provided for 400 persons by the spirited proprietors of the railway, but the hilarity of the occasion was much damped by the occurrence of a serious and fatal accident. Four waggons, in which there could not be less than from forty to fifty people, chiefly labourers connected with the railway, had just commenced the descent of the second inclined plane, when one of the shackles which attached the rope from the waggons suddenly snapped, and the waggons ran amain. When they approached the end

Planet locomotive, of the same type as the first locomotive acquired by the S&TR and named *Thomas Newcomen*. (Beamish Museum)

4 *Newcastle Courant*, 18 May 1834

of the incline, which is nearly a mile in length, they had acquired a considerable degree of velocity, and too great praise cannot be bestowed on the man at the engine stationed at the top of the first incline, who, with great presence of mind, by changing the slip, and thus interposing four loaded waggons which were lying on the sideway, effectually prevented the waggons which were running amain from rushing down the first incline. We regret to add, that by the shock caused by the waggons coming in contact, one man was killed, and a boy, nine years of age, so seriously injured, that he died during the night. Several others had bones fractured by leaping off the waggons during their descent, and some received contusions.[5]

The tragic accident on the Weatherhill incline, coming to its conclusion at the head of Crawleyside, marred what should have been great celebrations for the opening of the first half of the railway. Unfortunately, in the 1830s, railway accidents were commonplace, and the history of the S&TR is pockmarked with similar incidents. Work on the more

View down Weatherhill incline, towards Crawleyside, where the fatal opening day runaway commenced (the original engineman's cottage in the centre of the photograph marks the head of Crawleyside incline and the stationary engine house).

5 *Newcastle Courant*, 24 May 1834

profitable section of the line, bringing the coal down for export, was still ongoing. In June 1834, the foundation stone for the outer wall of the dock being built at South Shields for the railway was laid by the resident director, William Harrison. The laying of the stone was 'amid the tremendous cheers of the workmen and a great number of spectators, and the discharge of cannon'. After giving a speech, Harrison and the large party of gentlemen at the ceremony dined at the Golden Lion 'where the evening was spent in a spirit of the greatest hilarity'.[6] This outer wall was one of the major curtailments of the S&TR owing to mounting costs, never being built. The coal drops themselves, which were vital for the movement of coal, were of exceptional quality. An advantage of the S&TR design was that the 'vibrating frame' (the frame that carried the wagon on to lower it over the hold of the ship, at which point the bottom of the wagon would be opened and its contents discharged) pivoted at the bottom of the drops rather than in the middle, and was 54.5 feet long, meaning it had a longer reach, enabling ships to be loaded even at low water on a spring tide.

The remaining section of the line from Annfield Plain to South Shields was opened on 10 September 1834. Fortunately, there was nothing more significant than rain to dampen the celebrations this time. One hundred wagons of coal were received at South Shields from the company's Medomsley Colliery and shipped aboard the brig *Sally*. The directors and other guests were transported in a 'handsome car' drawn by what was reported as a small engine, likely Planet type locomotive *Thomas Newcomen*.

The coal drops at South Shields on the opening of the S&TR, September 1834. (Tyne & Wear Museums/Bridgeman Images)

---

6 *Newcastle Courant*, 28 June 1834

CHAPTER 3

Running the Railway

Aside from the S&TR's collieries, which at the time of opening were not fully working, in 1834 just three collieries – Tanfield Moor, Waldridge and Washington – agreed to send their coal via the railway. In November 1834 the first coal was brought down from Waldridge Colliery. In one day, 19.5 keels worth of coal (around 410 tonnes) were transported the 13 miles to the quay at South Shields, and in two hours was loaded onto the *Favourite* of South Shields. To mark the occasion, the owners of Waldridge Colliery treated the resident directors of the S&TR and several friends to a night of entertainment at the Golden Lion Inn.[7]

The maintenance of the line was done by contractors who received a set amount per mile to keep the line and lineside in good condition, the contract also stipulating that they must clear 'all snowfalls not exceeding three inches in depth and assisting the company to clear the heavier falls'. There was no signalling at the commencement of the railway – engines

Late 1830s view of Waldridge Colliery by Thomas Harrison Hair.

---

7   *Newcastle Courant,* 29 November 1834

were equipped with a tin lamp containing two candles as a form of headlight (to give visible warning a train was coming, rather than give any real improvement in visibility for the engine crew). A trial was made with an oil lamp said to have been invented by a local sailor:

> In order that the new lamp should have a fair trial, the inventor was allowed to make an experimental trip with one, on the hindmost waggon of a train, but the jolting and bumping speedily dislodged both inventor and invention.[8]

Signalling certainly came into effect later in the S&TR's life when the junction with the Brandling Junction Railway at Brockley Whins was created, the signalling there – or lack of – resulting in an accident in 1839 described later.

In April 1835 it was announced by the S&TR[9] that they were now leading Stanhope lime and that 'a regular supply will now be kept up at' Whitelea Head, White Hall or Cold Rowley, Watling Street, Medomsley (preparations were being made for a depot here), Greencroft, Durham Turnpike, Boldon and South Shields.

The sale of lime got off to a good start: fifty to sixty chaldrons of lime a day were sent from the kilns at Stanhope. A large set of six limekilns were constructed adjacent to the line at Bantling Castle in 1835 to increase lime production, which unlike the kilns at Crawleyside, had access to coal pits nearby. The impressive structure, built in a convex

1835 limekilns at Bantling Castle, near Annfield Plain.

8 Hodgson, G. B., *The Borough of South Shields: From the Earliest Period to the Close of the Nineteenth Century* (Newcastle: Andrew Reid & Co., 1903), pp. 386–387

9 *Newcastle Courant*, 11 April 1835

Close-up view of the inscription on the 1835 limekilns. (Beamish Museum)

curve, is fortunate to still exist, mostly in good condition apart from No. 3 arch, which has collapsed. Reputedly, mortar using lime from these limekilns was used to build Newcastle Central station in the 1840s.

The landsale of coal and lime by the railway was used in advertising – an 1835 advert for the letting of an estate at Consett keen to point out that 'the above property is advantageously situated by the Proximity to the Stanhope and Tyne Railroad, by which lime and coal can be procured at a reasonable Expense'.[10] There was a benefit to being even closer to the line. An 1841 advert for auction of a farm at Leadgate, where the line ran through the farmland, earnt the owner £1 13s annually in wayleaves, as well as giving 'a facility for the carriage of Lime to the Land' and, courtesy of this part of the line being worked by horses, free manure!'[11]

The London offices of the railway were at No. 26 New Broad Street, London, with the company headquarters at South Shields and TE Harrisons Engineers' Office at No. 6 Salem Street. Among Harrison's staff who helped in building the line was a Mr F. Charlton, who went on to become surveyor to the county of Northumberland.[12] Engine building and repairing shops were on Salem Street, later becoming used as stables by South Shields Corporation and later a cab company until demolished in 1900 to construct the west entrance for the NER passenger station. Next to the engine works was the station house for conducting goods and passenger business. Passenger business was very limited as the main purpose of the railway was, of course, the carriage of coal and limestone. Passengers

---

10 *Newcastle Courant*, 5 December 1835

11 *Newcastle Courant*, 25 June 1841

12 *Newcastle Courant*, 15 April 1881

The Stanhope & Tyne
Railroad Company
Landsale Coal and
Lime Depot of 1834
at West Boldon,
now relocated at
Beamish Museum.
(Beamish Museum)

Left: Close-up of the inscription of the coal and lime depot in situ at West Boldon. (Beamish Museum)

Below: View of West Boldon, after the rails had been removed, showing the coal and lime depot with the path of the track leading up to it. The S&TR continued left past the station house towards South Shields. (Beamish Museum)

started to be carried from April 1835 onwards, following requests from the poor asking for permission to ride in coal wagons. The company initially agreed when application was made but a more suitable solution came about. An open carriage with low sides and benches for seats was attached to the rear of coal trains and ran between South Shields and the Durham turnpike road (where connection could be made with stagecoaches for the north and south). Later a carriage was run on its own with the locomotive once a fortnight on pay days, but later ran several times a day. A 1903 description told how it

> ran at first three and afterwards four times each way daily, between South Shields and the Durham turnpike, where passengers could take the mail coaches to Durham or Newcastle or beyond. The 'coach' was an open truck with low sides, resembling the goods waggons in use to-day, with seats placed in it and a door on each side. The whole 'passenger department' was represented by a single official, who was guard, porter, booking-clerk, ticket-collector, and station-master all in one, and who travelled with the train. The 'tickets' were tin 'checks'.[13]

This was done at a loss to the company, but, against the advice of T. E. Harrison, the directors wanted to continue it as a public service. In the first four months of 1839, 4,325

Station,
outh Shields.

A 1905 view of South Shields station on approximately the site of the original S&TR headquarters. This station opened in 1879, replacing the former Low Shields station on the Brandling Junction Railway line. (Beamish Museum)

---

13 Hodgson, G. B., *The Borough of South Shields: From the Earliest Period to the Close of the Nineteenth Century* (Newcastle: Andrew Reid & Co., 1903), p. 386

The overbridge at Birtley, crossing the Great North Road (later the A1, and now the A167). In 1834 the railway was on a level crossing over the road, and this was the terminus of passenger carrying with stagecoaches met on the road here. The Wheatsheaf Inn, visible just under the bridge on the left, was no doubt welcomed by the passengers. The level crossing was replaced by a bridge here in 1857, the current bridge dating from the late nineteenth century.

passengers were carried, bringing in £177, 6s and 11d.[14] Goods were also carried, but again traffic was very limited, bringing in just 4 per cent of revenue.

By 1835 there were three coal drops in use on the quayside at South Shields, with plans to build more (curiously the print of the opening of the line shows five in place). Heavy gales in January 1835 led to the ring of a mooring buoy off the S&TR's coal drops at South Shields breaking off and causing four ships to break adrift, including the *Atlas* of Dundee, which received considerable damage.[15]

The unusual – to modern minds – habit of 'industrial tourism' was partaken in by Sir George Head, who published his travels across the country in the two volume *Home Tour Through the Manufacturing Districts*. His tour of England in 1835 took in the sight of the coal drops of the S&TR at South Shields, describing them as of 'unusual magnitude' and that they 'claim the merit of being superior to any in England'. His account of the coal drops is worth quoting in verbatim:

> Their site, at a short distance from the mouth of the Tyne, is elevated so considerably above the river, that the main beam, or jib of the drop, is 55 feet in length; the pivot, instead of being in the middle of the jib, as is the case at Middleborough, where the balancing weights

14 *The Railway Times* Volume 2, No. 97, 9 November 1839
15 *Caledonian Mercury*, 24 January 1835

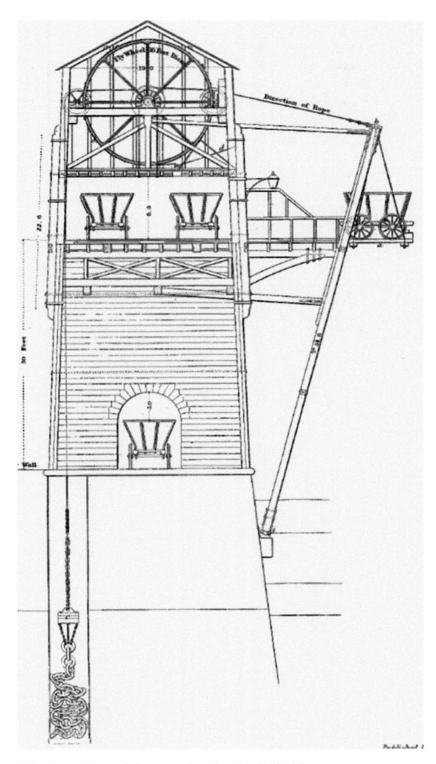

Side view of the coal drops employed at South Shields.

act upon the opposite extremity, is here at the bottom, therefore it is raised and lowered after the manner of a ladder. An engine house is built above the drop, from which flat ropes are fixed to a crossbar at the top of the jib. The machinery within the engine house consists of a cast-iron fly wheel, 16 feet in diameter, appended to the axis on which the ropes are wound: the laden wagon swings on the crossbar, and as it descends the balancing weight of five tonnes ascends to the summit of the drop, the balancing weight sinks again into the shaft, of which, by-the-way, the latter being partly filled with water, the action must be attended with diminished effect; however, no doubt it is adjusted accordingly. The peculiar description of this weight is admirably calculated to act equably, so as to avoid any jar or jerk, which might otherwise injure or break the machinery, and at all events be attended with bad effect; the identical principle is here applied, as in the tail of a boy's kite; a great part consisting of enormous rings or links of iron, which being raised from the ground one after another, destroy the effect of oscillation, without diminishing the power of gravity. I was informed that each circular link of this massive chain, of which there are a score or more, weighed two and a half hundredweight; I hastily measured one, and found it to be sixteen inches in circumference, and eleven inches and a half across the inner diameter.

The effect is grand, standing in a convenient position, to see and hear this enormous mechanical power in action: first, the wagon, weighing, together with its load, four tonnes, not reckoning the frame or cradle on which it stands, and two men beside it, altogether slowly descending from a height of upward 50 feet, down upon the deck of the vessel below; and with the sweep of a radius of 55 feet, describing its graceful periphery in the air, as is the stupendous bulk of the counterbalancing chain is dragged upward, as it were reluctantly, with a writing motion. The creaking and groaning of timber, the stress on the machinery, the grating of the brake, the rattling of the huge links, the clash of the hammer against iron bolts, and the thundering crash of the coal falling through the bottom of the wagon into the hold of the vessel, are all sounds the excite the senses and rivet the attention; while a farther source of contemplation arises by thinking that the same operation is repeated over and over again during every working day throughout the year, and yet, after all that, the whole establishment altogether is but as a speck in the balance, compared with the vast, incessant shipments that cross the bar of the Tyne, whose banks on either side, the whole distance from Newcastle, are studded with chimneys. These vomit into the air a dense mass of smoke, till nature herself seems, as it were, forced to take again under her special charge, in the form of one huge, black, unbroken cloud, the noxious particles and effluvia rejected by the saturated atmosphere.[16]

A more technical description given by T. E. Harrison described the use of the drops:

One of these drops is capable of shipping one Newcastle chaldron of coals of 53 cwt. every minute, but this is never required in practice, as the coals cannot be 'trimmed' in the ships so fast, the usual work being from 25 to 35 chaldrons per hour of operation. The waggon being placed upon the cradle and the cradle being released from the gangway by taking out the pin, the brakesman eases the brake from the brake wheel by raising the handle,

---

16 Head, Sir G., *A Home Tour Through the Manufacturing Districts of England in the Summer of 1835* (New York: Harper & Brothers, 1836), pp. 277–9

An 1835 image of a typical chaldron wagon as used on the S&TR. Constructed by contractors and hired to the railway and consisting of a wooden body with iron wheels, they weighed 30 cwt (1,524 kgs) with a carrying capacity of 53 cwt (2,692 kgs), which was loaded from the top and emptied through bottom doors. Note the brake gear and man on the back, required to ride the chaldrons on inclines and brake them as necessary. (Beamish Museum)

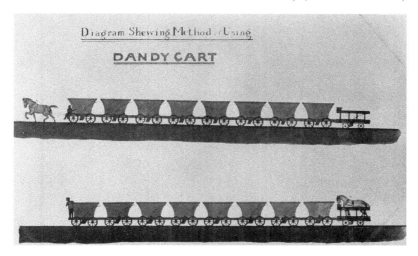

Diagram showing the use of Dandy Carts, used on the horse-worked section between the foot of Nanny Mayer's incline and the south-western side of Hownes Gill. Horses rode in the Dandy Cart at the rear of the wagons for the 2 miles from Healeyfield Bridge, through Rowley, to the top of Hownes Gill incline. The train moved using gravity, although the horse had to pull the cart and wagons back up the slight gradient on the return. This image shows a Dandy Cart in use on the Stockotn & Darlington Railway, who pioneered their use. There is no known image showing what a Dandy Cart on the S&TR looked like. (Beamish Museum)

and the vibrating frame, with the waggon suspended in the cradle, begins by its gravity to descend. As the waggon descends, the counter-balance ring weights are gradually lifted from the bottom of the well, the rope sustaining them winding on to the sheave, as the ropes sustaining the vibrating frame are unwound from the sheaves. The waggon having arrived at the proper point, and the coals being discharged into the vessel by a man who descends with the waggon for that purpose, the counterbalance weight has then the preponderance, and by its gravity brings the vibrating frame and light waggon back to its original position. The weight of the counterbalance is so nicely adjusted, that either the loaded waggon in its descent, or the light waggon ascending, will move at any angle at which they may have stopped. The brakesman has also ample power to stop the waggon at any point he may require, or even, in case of accident to the counterbalance weights, to hold the loaded waggon suspended. The general arrangement of the whole differs from that of any drops erected either upon the Tyne or Wear.[17]

The coal that was being sent down to London was marketed at the general public as well as the great industries that required feeding. The Medomsley Coal Company advertised in London papers that there would be a constant supply of their coal in London, owing to the contract with the S&TR who were delivering them to Whiting's Wharf on Broad Street, Ratcliff. The coal sold to the public was delivered straight from the ship, large and screened, to any address in London for cash on delivery. Medomsley W. E. coal was sold at 28 shillings per ton, Lanchester W. E. coal at a shilling less per ton. Confidently, the advert stated, 'A single trial will convince the consumer of the economy of using these coals.'[18]

In September 1835, a report was published from a trial at the Durham Assizes (a court held twice a year, usually one in February and one in August) between the S&TR and a plaintiff – a wines and spirits merchant – in South Shields wanting compensation owing to the effects of trains running near his property, ruining the goods he was selling and otherwise making his life a misery. A witness was examined

who stated that he lived close to the Railway, that the vibration, though slight, was not annoying, that his bed-room was so near the arch over which it passed that he could step out of the window upon it. The witness also stated that the engines passed within 4 feet of his bed without disturbing him, and that he had placed a tumbler of water on his parlour table to observe the vibration, which did not exceed that which was caused by the passing of ordinary vehicles.

Despite this evidence in favour of the railway, the complainant was awarded £104 from the S&TR.

Aside from the danger of wagons running away, as on the opening day tragedy at Weatherhill, the rope (and later wire) and chain attached to the wagons on inclines had the

17 Harrison, T. E., 'Description of the Drops used by the Stanhope and Tyne Railroad Company for the Shipment of Coals at South Shields' in *Transactions of the Institution of Civil Engineers* Volume 2, Issue 1, 1838

18 *Morning Post*, 13 June 1835

potential to seriously injure or kill. Such an incident happened in September 1836, when Joseph Sopwith was withdrawing a bolt from a wagon near to the winding engine at Flats Lane. While doing so he was 'caught by the chain', suggesting that he was withdrawing the bolt holding the chain while the chain was still at tension. The effect of the chain catching him was that 'his body was nearly cut in two. He died almost instantly. The deceased has left a widow and eight children'.[19]

Presentation of fine gifts to railway employees became a long-standing tradition, and an early retiree from the S&TR was surely one of the earliest recipients of this in early 1837. John Granger, retiring from the post of resident agent of the company at Annfield Plain (described as the S&TR's central station), was presented with a fine silver snuff box by his friends in the local area.[20]

Several years into the operation of the S&TR, by and large everything was still looking good so far as the shareholders saw it. It was announced in September 1837 that, for the year ending 31 December 1836, a dividend of £5 per share was to be issued, the same as the previous year. However, despite this apparent sign of success, in both cases the dividend was paid from a loan, belying a serious financial issue, which, however successful the S&TR was to be in its movement of minerals, outlined the railway's precarious existence.[21, 22]

Trackbed from Hog Hill Tunnel looking south towards the end of Crawleyside incline and the limekiln and quarry.

19 *The Times*, 7 September 1836 (quoted from the *Durham Chronicle*)
20 *Newcastle Courant*, 13 January 1837
21 *Morning Chronicle*, 16 September 1837
22 *The Times*, 23 June 1836

CHAPTER 4

Locomotives

The first S&TR locomotive placed on the rails in May 1834 was Robert Stephenson & Co. No. 31 *Thomas Newcomen*, one of the highly successful Planet type locomotives with a 2-2-0 arrangement. Although Stephenson's world-famous *Rocket* is widely known as the first modern locomotive, the slightly later Planet type more closely fit that accolade with the smokebox and firebox integral to the main boiler unit, a proper set of frames acting as a chassis, as well as, like *Rocket*, having a multitube boiler. The motion was improved too, with the cylinders arranged inside the frames and the pistons working on a crank axle to drive the wheels. The Planet type ordered by the S&TR was named *Thomas Newcomen*, and most of the other S&TR locomotives had names of men related to steam or the S&TR. The small Planet type seems – with the benefit of hindsight – an odd choice for a line built to move minerals, as they were better suited for lighter services such as fast goods or passenger services, and the passenger services operated by the S&TR were very small scale and not originally envisaged.

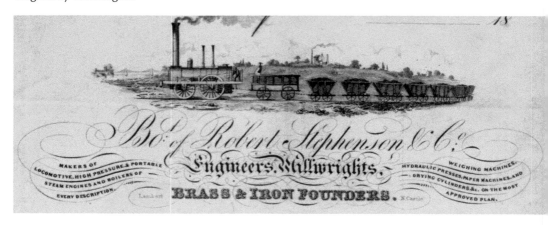

Header of a letter from Robert Stephenson & Co. showing a Planet type locomotive hauling a coal train. The letter was regarding the supply of ironwork for the S&TR's bridges at South Shields.

A more suitable Stephenson locomotive for the S&TR was acquired next and became the most common type used on the line. An improvement of the Planet type, the Samson was similar in appearance but with a 0-4-0 wheel arrangement, therefore with all four wheels coupled together and better suited for moving heavy trains. Next came the Large Samson with 0-4-2 wheel arrangement with four coupled wheels of 4-foot 6-inch diameter and two rear trailing carrying wheels of 3-foot 6-inch diameter, allowing for a larger, more powerful, boiler to be carried. The first Large Samson was built for the S&TR as Stephenson works No. 36 but was ready before the S&TR was, so was instead delivered to the Leicester & Swannington Railway. Not all the Large Samsons ordered by S&TR were built by Stephenson's. Potentially, like the stationary engines, the order was split with other manufacturers to get them delivered as soon as possible.

Barely a month after the full length of the line had been opened, an advert for the sale, by private contract, of a locomotive used on the line appeared. The advertisement, posted on 22 October 1834, stated 'A Valuable and powerful Locomotive STEAM ENGINE, nearly new, having been only a short Time in Use on the Stanhope and Tyne Railroad, at the East End of the Line, where it can now be inspected.' The contacts were Messrs Barker & Son of North Shields and Messrs Bainbridge and Sparrier of South Shields. This was

Fine view of S&TR Large Samson type locomotive *John Buddle*, built in 1834 by Robert Stephenson & Co. (National Railway Museum/Science & Society Picture Library)

likely a contractor's engine, rather than one owned and used by the company itself, of unknown type.[23]

While the locomotives were mostly of the same type, and all fitted with tenders for the coal and water, as usual for the period, there would still be differences in the smaller details as they were hand-built. As well as the S&TR records, surviving records from the manufacturers supplemented by railway literature of the period – notably Francis Whishaw's *The Railways of Great Britain and Ireland Practically Described and Illustrated* (1840) – has helped build information regarding them. Aside from *Thomas Newcomen*, as mentioned, most locomotives were of the Large Samson class. The Bedlington and S&TR-built six-coupled locomotives were of unknown appearance, but locomotive *George Stephenson* was a six-coupled Large Samson, identical to *William Hutchinson* apart from the wheel arrangement.

It is especially unfortunate that it is not known what *Projector* looked like, the only known locomotive built by the S&TR. Further locomotives were certainly built at the

Known locomotives of the Stanhope & Tyne Railroad Company					
Name	Built	Manufacturer	Works Number	Wheel Arrangement	Cylinders
Thomas Newcomen	1834	Robert Stephenson & Co.	31	2-2-0	11-inch diameter × 18-inch stroke
John Buddle	1834	Robert Stephenson & Co.	50	0-4-2	14-inch diameter × 18-inch stroke
Nathaniel Ogle	1834	Robert Stephenson & Co.	63	0-4-2	14-inch diameter × 18-inch stroke
James Watt	1834	Robert Stephenson & Co.	66	0-4-2	14-inch diameter × 18-inch stroke
Jacob Perkins	1835	Charles Tayleur	14	0-4-2	14-inch diameter × 18-inch stroke
TE Harrison	1835	R & W Hawthorns		0-4-2	14-inch diameter × 18-inch stroke
Michael Longridge	1837	Bedlington Iron Works	104	0-6-0	14-inch diameter × 18-inch stroke
Robert Stephenson	1834 or 1835	Robert Stephenson & Co.	94	Unknown	Unknown
William Hutchinson	1838	Robert Stephenson & Co.	155	0-4-2	15-inch diameter × 18-inch stroke
George Stephenson	1839	Robert Stephenson & Co.	156	0-6-0	15-inch diameter × 18-inch stroke
Projector	1839	Stanhope & Tyne Railroad Company	1	0-6-0	15-inch diameter × 18-inch stroke

---

23 *Newcastle Courant*, 1 November 1834

South Shields workshops as per the first-hand accounts of George Hardy, who worked there during its tenure by the York, Newcastle & Berwick Railways, testify, locomotive production ceasing in 1854. It is not known if any further locomotives were built at South Shields during the remaining existence of the S&TR or for the Pontop & South Shields Railway. *Projector* was also the only confirmed S&TR locomotive not named after a person.

An additional locomotive is listed by Whishaw, *Robert Hawthorn*, built by Robert Stephenson & Co. but with no other information. As the locomotive does not exist in any of the Stephenson records it is possible this is just an error.

The locomotive working records for 1835, 1836 and 1837 are still in existence[24] and are the most important of the very few official documents from the S&TR remaining. Not only does it confirm which locomotives were in use at that time, but also gives them fleet numbers on the 1836 sheet and details how busy they were. Interestingly, the records split the number of trips worked into two types – 9-mile trips or 8-mile trips. The length of the line worked by locomotives was 9.25 miles so presumably the 9-mile trips were moving coal from the foot of the last incline to South Shields. The 8-mile trips could be from a source closer to South Shields, potentially to the junction with the Durham Junction Railway. As early as May 1834, before either railway had opened, the Durham Junction Railway had

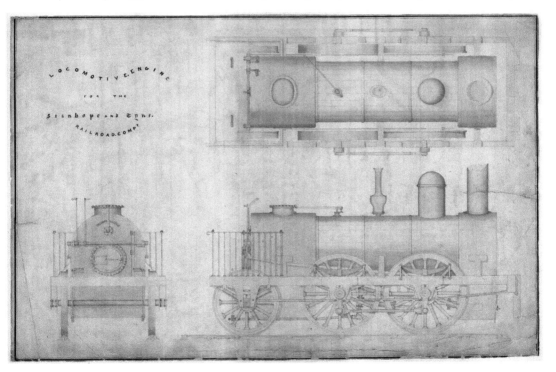

Works drawing of S&TR Large Samson type locomotive *TE Harrison*, built in 1835 by Hawthorns. (Tyne & Wear Museums/Bridgeman Images)

---

24 The National Archives RAIL 663/6 Stanhope and Tyne Rail-Road Company Locomotive and Rolling Stock Records

made an agreement with the S&TR to use the S&TR's locomotives.[25] This record taking does not seem to make any note or allowance for any shorter workings, if any were made, or passenger workings. The numbering of the locomotives according to the records was not chronological regarding the date the locomotives were delivered to the S&TR and may have started from 1836 when they first appear on the sheets.

1 January 1835 to 31 December 1835					
Locomotive No.	Locomotive Name	Days worked	Total number of journeys	9-mile journeys	8-mile journeys
1	Jacob Perkins	112	390	306	84
2	Robert Stephenson	212	743	618	125
3	James Watt	140	520	412	108
4	Nathaniel Ogle	244	876	673	203
5	John Buddle	181	595	478	117
6	TE Harrison	68	235	207	28
7	Thomas Newcomen	93	374	294	80
	Total	1050	3833		

1 January 1836 to 31 December 1836					
Locomotive No.	Locomotive Name	Days worked	Total number of journeys	9-mile journeys	8-mile journeys
1	Jacob Perkins	239	869	671	198
2	Robert Stephenson	223	843	712	131
3	James Watt	197	709	554	155
4	Nathaniel Ogle	144	558	469	89
5	John Buddle	140	543	439	104
6	TE Harrison	139	535	445	90
7	Thomas Newcomen	78	315	313	2
	Total	1160	4372		

25 Tomlinson, W. W., *The North Eastern Railway, Its Rise and Development* (Newcastle: Andrew Reid & Co., 1914), p. 225

1 January 1837 to 31 December 1837					
Locomotive No.	Locomotive Name	Days worked	Total number of journeys	9-mile journeys	8-mile journeys
1	Jacob Perkins	200	746	603	143
2	Robert Stephenson	230	880	760	120
3	James Watt	213	939	790	149
4	Nathaniel Ogle	135	465	373	92
5	John Buddle	188	668	518	150
6	TE Harrison	196	722	555	167
7	Thomas Newcomen	90	368	255	113
	Total	**1252**	**4788**		

The locomotives seem to have worked well enough and been capable of what was asked of them. Powerful for their day, the locomotives could, in bad weather, 'always take twenty-eight waggons, either loaded, upon the level; or empty, up the gradient of 1 in 211'. The usual load was thirty-two wagons, or up to forty in good weather with dry rails where adhesion was at its best.[26]

In 1838, T. E. Harrison gave information regarding the fuel and fireboxes of the locomotives on the S&TR:

From long experience it was found that coal, which contained much bitumen, caused the tubes of the fire-boxes to leak in a very short time. They obtained coal as free from sulphur as possible, and the consequences had been most advantageous; for during two years and a half, not more than one hundred and twenty tubes had been required for seven engines, of which four were always at work. The tubes were of copper, and 1 5/8-inch in diameter. The usual speed was about 10 miles an hour. One engine weighing 10 tonnes, on six wheels, conveyed 128 tonnes of coal. The consumption of fuel was 2 1/10 lb of coal, per ton of goods, per mile. The gross load was more than double the weight of the goods. The cheapness at which they were able to carry goods was to be attributed to the low speed.

Among the autobiography of George Hardy, who went on to work on the Londonderry Railway for forty-seven years (finishing as manager of the line), is his eyewitness account of the S&TR at work:

I saw the commencement to make the line at the low end and two engines Nos 1 and 2, each with 4 wheels coupled dragging the wagons laden with ballast from the Hill, other two

26 Woods, N., *A Practical Treatise on Rail-roads* (London: Longman, Orme, Brown, Green, 1838), pp. 475–476

View of the Bedlington Iron Works, where the boilers for the Stephenson-built S&TR locomotives were built as well as S&TR locomotive *Michael Longridge*.

engines were also on the place, one by Hackworth, Stockton and another by Shildon works. When fairly opened there was many other engines chiefly from Bedlington Iron Works.[27]

The account is not quite accurate owing to its claim regarding Bedlington Iron Works when only one of the known fleet was built there – although the boilers for the Stephenson-built engines were made at Bedlington, which may be what Hardy was referring to or confused with. A list of S&TR locomotives stated by Hardy interestingly includes three not in any known fleet list – *Earl Percy, W. Williams* and what appears to be, from what can be deduced from his handwriting, *Algernon*, which may have been later S&TR locomotives.

W. W. Tomlinson's *The North Eastern Railway* mentions eight S&TR locomotives were built by Stephenson (seven are known for definite, the eighth could be an error including the supposed *Robert Hawthorn*), with the others built by Tayleur, Hawthorn, Longridge & Co. (Bedlington Iron Works), the S&TR itself and Hackworth & Downing. Tomlinson also states, quoting the notes of Jos Stephenson, the S&TR locomotives were painted slate colour, which does seem discernible in the grey colour of the frames on the painting of *John Buddle* (the green tinge to the wooden boiler cladding is likely discolouration over the years, and would presumably have been a natural wood colour).

The relatively flat levels around Medomsley (2.25 miles between East Carr House incline foot and west Loud Bank incline foot) and Stanley (2.5 miles between east Loud Bank incline foot and Stanley bank incline), which were originally worked by horse, were suitable for locomotives. In December 1838 a notice was issued by T. E. Harrison looking for 'persons willing to contract for the finding and working of Locomotive Engines, for the Conveyance of Coals,

---

27 Beamish Museum Collections LIB3428, Autobiography of George Hardy, Seaham Harbour, 1825–1917

Lime, and other Articles upon the Stanley and Medomsley Levels'.[28] In George B. Hodgson's *The Borough of South Shields*, published in 1903, it is claimed that 'one of Hackworth's earliest locomotives, the *Experiment*, built at Shildon, worked one of the levels, and *Blucher*, built at Stockton, another.'[29] These would match George Hardy's account of seeing two Hackworth locomotives working on the line and the mention of them by W. W. Tomlinson. 'Experiment' could refer to the Stockton & Darlington Railway No. 6 *Experiment*, built in 1826 by George Stephenson, a four-wheel locomotive later rebuilt at Shildon as a six-wheeler. 'Blucher' does not match any known Hackworth engine but there are very few records remaining of the Thomas Hackworth and later Fossick & Hackworth works at Stockton.

The wagons used were standard chaldron wagons in use by other railways at the time and had been on the horse-drawn waggonways for many years before. The chaldrons used on the S&TR were hired in from contractors, the S&TR being responsible for repair costs. A chaldron was a unit of measurement. In the Newcastle area, this was equivalent to 53-hundredweight (just over 2.5 metric tonnes). The wagons, wooden bodied with cast iron wheels, were loaded from the top and discharged from doors in the bottom. This design of top loading and bottom discharging was standard for the carrying of coal and other minerals in the North East, being developed through the nineteenth and twentieth centuries with carrying capacity increasing. Empty, the chaldron wagons weighed 30-hundredweight. Another name was added to the list of those killed or maimed on the S&TR in July 1838. Joseph Rowe, while stepping onto wagons near Stanhope in July 1838, 'missed his hold and was thrown under the wheels'. The wheels nearly severed his

Stockton & Darlington Railway locomotive *Experiment* as rebuilt as a six-wheeler, which possibly later worked on the S&TR.

28 *Newcastle Courant*, 14 December 1838
29 Hodgson, George B., *The Borough of South Shields: From the Earliest Period to the Close of the Nineteenth Century* (Newcastle: Andrew Reid & Co., 1903), p. 385

Oxhill Crossing in Stanley on the Stanley level, seen in 1921. Despite an attempt by the local council in the 1900s to get this major disruption to road traffic replaced by a bridge, the crossing on the original S&TR line was kept open until the 1970s to serve Morrison Busty pit at Annfield Plain. (Beamish Museum)

leg from his body. Men nearby soon rendered assistance, but he passed away soon after, leaving a wife and child.[30]

Steam locomotives and their constituent parts are consumable items, and as the locomotives were always used with the heaviest load possible (to make best use of them), wear on the wheels of the locomotives was, by way of comparison, higher than that of other railways.[31] With the cylinders and valve gear being inside the frames of the locomotive, underneath of the boiler, it was found that most of the expense in repairing the locomotives was in labour expended in disassembling the locomotive. To avoid the need for this, T. E. Harrison designed a new type of locomotive where the boiler was on a separate chassis to the cylinders and driving wheels and connected by a 'steam-tight universal joint'.[32] This bizarre design was patented by Harrison, and two were built by Hawthorn's for the Great Western Railway, where their large single driving wheels met Isambard Kingdom Brunel's specifications for locomotives with a high speed but low cylinder stroke speed. The two locomotives were named *Thunderer* and *Hurricane* and worked for just over a year.

Aside from the dry technical details of the locomotives and mystery around which others existed on the S&TR, other than working slow coal trains the main interest regarding their

30 *Champion*, 29 July 1838

31 Woods, N., A Practical Treatise on Rail-roads (London: Longman, Orme, Brown, Green, 1838), p. 480

32 Woods, N., A practical treatise on rail-roads (London: Longman, Orme, Brown, Green, 1838), p. 614

1838 view of an S&TR Large Samson locomotive.

histories comes from the grislier side of railway history – the locomotives involved in incidents and accidents.

Death and injuries on the railways weren't purely from the dangers of the working conditions. One engineman was put on trial at the Durham Summer Assizes, in 1839, for the death of a platelayer occurring on the morning of Tuesday 4 June 1839, on the line between Boldon and Fatfield. A locomotive had come to a stop on the line between Fatfield and Boldon to take on water at the Don station house and, while stationary, twenty-year-old engineman Thomas Smith was raking the ashes from the firebox. While doing so, platelayer John Alderson came up to the locomotive and apparently without warning struck Smith on the head with his hand. Smith said he would strike Alderson if he did it again, and Alderson did, knocking Smith's cap off. Smith then hit Alderson on the head with the iron coal rake Smith was using and had in hand but was not sure whether it was the teeth of the rake that hit Alderson. Alderson shouted 'oh dear' and went into the station house. Four men – Smith and the other engineman named Dixon, William Winter, who was witness at the trial, and Alderson's brother – went after Alderson, and Smith offered him some cotton waste to wipe his head with. Alderson refused at first but upon Smith offering again, Alderson accepted. Alderson then raised his fist and threatened Smith but did not strike him. Smith and Dixon then went away on the engine, and Winter put Alderson on his way to a surgeon to see to the wound. The wound was bleeding heavily but when Winter last saw Alderson he still appeared strong and not tipsy at all. Alderson's body was later found in a ditch that ran by the side of the road, several hundred yards from the station, by a girl on her way to school, who saw Alderson's cap lying in the road and then his body in the ditch. The body was face downwards in the water, which was only a few inches deep and so did not cover the head, and his arms crossed over his chest. A surgeon at West Boldon examined the body and decided that the wound on the head was 'sufficient to cause death'. The judge, however, was decided that the wound was insufficient to cause death if 'proper means had been taken to staunch the blood'. The judge stopped the case as death was likely caused by suffocation rather than by the wound itself. While the wounding of Alderson by Smith had been severe – perhaps unintentionally – it was in response to the unprovoked repeated assault by Alderson and it may be that the judge was lenient owing to this.[33, 34]

In the late 1830s, a new railway – the Brandling Junction Railway – was constructed, which ran from Gateshead to Sunderland and to South Shields. In running east to west, it crossed the S&TR on the level, north of Boldon, at a location called Brockley Whins. Writing on the Brandling Junction Railway in 1840, Francis Whishaw describes how the

greatest error, however, committed in laying out this work is the crossing on a level the Stanhope & Tyne Railway, a coal-line in full work, which is performed chiefly by powerful engines. How frightful the idea of a collision of two powerful engines travelling at considerable velocities, which frequently may occur without the most judicious of signals![35]

Level crossing at West Boldon in 1918. In the left foreground is the entrance to the coal and lime depot. The original S&TR line crosses to the right towards South Shields. (Beamish Museum)

33 *Newcastle Courant*, 7 June 1839

34 *Newcastle Courant*, 2 August 1839

35 Whishaw, F., *The Railways of Great Britain and Ireland Practically Described and Illustrated* (London: John Weale, 1942), p. 46

Such a collision occurred at Brockley Whins (Whishaw mentioned hearing of a collision occurring the last time he was in Newcastle but was unable to obtain details, so could have been the very same) one morning in October 1839. A man was stationed at the crossing to give signals to approaching trains but, despite this, reported as either being due to the signalmans neglect or the enginemen not taking notice, a Brandling Junction Railway train being pulled by the locomotive *Newcastle*, running from Wearmouth to South Shields, ran into the back of a train worked by the locomotive *TE Harrison* on the S&TR line heading to Fatfield. The locomotive on the Brandling Junction Railway reportedly ran into the rear tender of the S&TR locomotive 'carrying it off the line and shivering it to pieces' in one report, another stating that the train was being pulled by the locomotive and instead the collision 'threw part of the waggons off the line, and misplaced some of the rails of the railway which were, however, shortly replaced'.[36] Fortunately, there was no injury to the enginemen on either locomotive, and just one bruise reported on a passenger on the Brandling Junction train.[37]

The signalling regulations in place to protect Brockley Whins had a large margin for error. If a red flag was held up, Brandling Junction Railway trains were to stop before reaching the crossing, with S&TR trains to continue without stopping. Alternatively, if a white flag was held up, the S&TR train was to stop and the Brandling train to continue. If no flag was shown at all then the train was to assume it was clear to continue. In the aftermath of the accident a much more detailed set of instructions was issued, changing

NOTICE.

The Enginemen belonging the *Brandling Junction Railway* are ordered to stop the Train before reaching the Crossing, when the Red Flag is held up; and to pass without stopping when the White Flag is held up, or no Flag at all.

The Enginemen belonging the *Stanhope and Tyne Railroad* are ordered to stop the empty Trains when the White Flag is held up; and the loaded Train to proceed and not to stop at all, when the Red Flag is held up.

South Shields, June 17, 1839.

Alfred Johnson. Printer. 2, Thrift Street.

The original signalling arrangements from June 1839 for the crossing of the S&TR and the Brandling Junction Railway at Brockley Whins. It is easy to see how this could have caused an accident as happened later that year.

---

36 *Newcastle Courant*, 25 October 1839
37 *Northern Liberator*, 26 October 1839

RULES AND REGULATIONS

FOR THE

Enginemen of the Brandling Junction, and Stanhope and Tyne Trains, for passing the Crossings at Brockley Whins and Boldon Lane.

BRANDLING JUNCTION ENGINEMEN.

DAY SIGNALS.

In approaching the *Crossings* either in *going towards* Shields, Gateshead, or Wearmouth, *when the Engine reaches the First Post* with a White Flag upon it, the *Engineman to sound his Whistle,* and to continue to do so, at intervals, until he *sees the Signal Flag hoisted* at the *Crossing.*

When the Trains arrive at the Second Post marked "Half Speed," *the speed to be so checked* that the Train shall not go at more than the rate of *Six Miles an Hour,* and if the *Signal is hoisted for the Train to proceed,* the Engineman *to pass the Crossing* at that rate of speed only.

The Engineman, *in every case, to stop* at the *Third Post,* marked "Stop," unless *he sees a White Flag alone hoisted.*

And in *all cases* where *a White Flag is not hoisted,* or *if a Red Flag is hoisted,* or *if both Flags are hoisted and waved backwards and forwards,* the Engineman *to stop the Train* at the *Third Post,* and not on any account whatever *to pass the Crossing* until *a White Flag alone is hoisted.*

NIGHT SIGNALS.

The Engineman to observe the same rules as to *sounding the Whistle* at the first or Flag Post, and *checking the speed* at the Second Post, as during the Day.

The Engineman, *in every case, to stop* at the *Third Post* if no Light is seen, or *if the Light is alternately exhibited and darkened,* and not again *to proceed* until *a clear and steady Single Light is distinctly seen.*

And if on arriving at the *first* or Flag Post, a steady Single Light is seen, and such Light is exhibited until the Engine arrives at the *Third Post,* the Train then *to proceed* through the Crossing; but, in *every other case, unless the Light is so seen,* the Engineman *to stop the Train* at the *Third Post,* and only *to proceed* when *a single Light is distinctly seen.*

FOG SIGNALS.

In *all cases during a Fog,* or *when the Engineman cannot distinctly see the Signals at the Crossings,* he must, on arriving *at the Flag Post, sound his Whistle,* and continue doing so at intervals, until *he arrives at the Third Post,* where *in every instance he must stop.* He must then send his Fireman forward to the Signal Man for orders, and not, *on any account whatever,* move beyond the Post *until he receives orders by his Fireman to proceed,* when he must *pass the Crossing* at a very moderate speed.

STANHOPE AND TYNE ENGINEMEN.

DAY SIGNALS.—LOADED TRAINS.

When the Loaded Train arrives at the *First Post* with a *Red Flag* upon it, the Engineman *to sound his Whistle,* and to continue to do so at intervals until he *sees the Signal Flag hoisted* at the Crossing. *When the Train arrives at the Second Post* marked "Half Speed," *the speed to be so checked* that the Train shall not move at the rate of more than *Five Miles an Hour,* at which rate he *is to proceed through the Crossing, if the Red Flag is hoisted.* If *no Flag is hoisted,* or *if both a Red and White Flag is hoisted and waved back and forwards,* the Engineman, if possible, *to stop before he reaches the Crossing,* and not to move on *until he sees a Red Flag alone hoisted.*

EMPTY TRAINS.

When the Empty Train arrives at the First Post with a *Red Flag* upon it, the Engineman *to sound his Whistle ;* and to continue to do so, at intervals, until he *sees the Signal Flag hoisted* at the Crossing. *When the Train arrives at the Second Post* marked "Half Speed," *the Speed to be so checked* that the Train shall not move at more than *Five Miles an Hour ;* and *if the Signal is for the Train to proceed,* the Engineman *to pass the Crossing* at that rate of speed only. The Engineman, *in every case, to stop* at the *Third Post,* marked "Stop," unless *he sees a Red Flag alone hoisted.* And in *all cases* when *a Red Flag is not hoisted,*—or, *if a White Flag is hoisted,*—or, *if both Flags are hoisted and waved back and forward,* the Engineman *to stop the Train* at the *Third Post ;* and not, on any account whatever, *to pass the Crossing* until *a Red Flag alone is hoisted.*

NIGHT SIGNALS.—LOADED TRAINS.

The Engineman to observe the same Rules as to *sounding the Whistle* at the First or Flag Post, and *checking the Speed* at the Second Post, as during the day : and when he observes *a steady single light exhibited, to pass on through the Crossing without stopping.* But if, on arriving at the *First Post,* he *does not see a single steady Light,*—or, *if he sees the Light alternately exhibited and darkened,* he must then check the Speed, so as, if possible, *to come to a stand* before he reaches the Crossing, and only *to proceed* when *a clear and steady single light is distinctly seen.*

EMPTY TRAINS.

The Engineman to observe the same Rules as to *sounding the Whistle* at the First or Flag Post, and *checking the Speed* at the Second Post, as during the Day :—but, in *every case to stop* at the *Third Post,* if no Light is seen, or, *if the Light is alternately exhibited and darkened,* not again *to proceed* until *a clear and steady single light is distinctly seen.* And if, on arriving at the *First* or Flag Post, a steady single Light is seen, and such *light is exhibited* until the Engine arrives at the *Third Post,* the Train then *to proceed* through the Crossing; but *in every other case, unless the Light is so seen,* the Engineman *to stop* the Train at the *Third Post,* and only *to proceed* when *a single Light is distinctly seen.*

FOG SIGNALS.—BOTH LOADED AND EMPTY TRAINS.

In *all cases during a Fog,* or, *when the Engineman cannot distinctly see the Signals* at the Crossing, he must, on arriving *at the Flag Post, sound his Whistle,* and continue doing so, at intervals, until *he arrives at the Third Post,* where, *in every instance, he must stop.* He must then send his Fireman forward to the Signal Man for Orders, and not, on any account whatever, move beyond the Post *until he receives Orders by his Fireman to proceed,* when he must *pass the Crossing* at a very moderate speed.

In addition to these Signals, the Enginemen on all the Lines are instructed *to keep a good look out* on approaching the Crossing; and if they observe any of the other Enginemen *not obeying the proper Signals ;* or *if they have any doubt as to the Signals exhibited,* or as to the propriety of passing the Crossing, they must in every instance stop the Train at the *Third Post,* and *not proceed until the proper Signals are clearly and distinctly seen.*

R. W. BRANDLING, Esq. *Managing Director of the Brandling Junction Railway.*
WM. HARRISON, Esq. }
A. J. F. MARRECO, Esq. } *Managing Directors of the Stanhope and Tyne Railway.*

October 30th, 1839.

Newcastle-upon-Tyne : Printed at the Journal Office, 59, Grey-Street, by John Hernaman.

The revised signalling arrangements at Brockley Whins, dated 30 October 1839.

the regulations using a system of three posts on both lines and in both of their directions at which trains should run at certain speeds or be prepared to stop at depending on the flags given – or not given. The regulations also considered whether the S&TR coal trains were loaded or unloaded, which would greatly affect their stopping distances. After all there was no continuous braking, and no brake van at the end. Instead, someone, likely the fireman, would walk the length of the train and individually pin down the brakes of each coal wagon to slow or stop the train. The regulations also took into account whether it was day, night or foggy. The priority given to the long coal trains of the S&TR often meant the Brandling trains were held up. In a monthly meeting of the Brandling Junction Railway in December 1840, trains waiting for the S&TR trains to pass Brockley Whins were the cause of delay to five Brandling trains in the space of just seven days.

Many lives have been ruined or ended on railways owing to easily avoidable accidents – a simple trip or slip can have dire consequences in what can be a highly dangerous environment. In April 1840 a young fireman attempted to climb onto a locomotive while it was in motion but fell. The entire train of thirty loaded wagons ran over him, severely crushing one leg and the thigh of the other leg. He died later that day. Boiler explosions, of railway locomotives and static boilers, were common at this time due to various reasons, including manufacturing fault or locomotive crews holding down safety valves (designed to release steam above a certain pressure to avoid the pressure reaching an unsafe level, which may result in explosion) to get a bit more power out of the locomotive. A boiler explosion on the Pontop & South Shields Railway in May 1842 no doubt involved one of the locomotives originally worked by the S&TR just over a year beforehand. The newspaper reported the incident switches from the tragic to the trivial so swiftly and without remark that to the modern reader it almost appears comical:

A dreadful accident occurred at Annfield Plane, on the Stanhope and Tyne Railway, on Wednesday last. A locomotive engine was standing on the line, preparing to start, when the boiler exploded, and half of it was carried to a distance of at least seventy yards. The engineman and brakesman (the former named Thomas Shevil, and the latter Edward Riddell) were killed on the spot. Shevil's foot was blown off. A shopkeeper, named Clark, who was walking past, had his hat knocked off, but was not injured; and another man, who was standing close by, fortunately escaped unhurt.[38]

---

38 *Newcastle Courant*, 28 May 1842

CHAPTER 5

Last Years of the Stanhope & Tyne Railroad Company

Permission was given in August 1838 for the S&TR to erect 'three gears' at South Shields.[39] Presumably this referred to three coal drops sketched by T. E. Harrison in July and August[40], which were drops six, seven and eight. Once permission had been given, construction would have soon followed and was certainly completed by 1841. The numbering of them shows that by late July 1838 five drops were in operation. The growing quantity of coals being shipped from the Tyne reached a chokepoint at the limited number of coal drops in use, and discussions were held in January 1838 regarding a new dock for shipping coal. Congestion at the S&TR's coal drops resulted, 'notwithstanding all that had been done to obviate such things', in 'an accumulation of vessels, impatient to succeed to their turns, obstructing part of the water-way, and doing occasional mischief to each other'.[41] The inevitable frustration caused to waiting ships crews was possibly the reason for an act of violence in 1839, which resulted in master mariner John Hutchinson being given a penalty of 40 shillings plus costs for assaulting Robert Galilee, the superintendent of the S&TR's coal drops at South Shields.[42] Despite involvement of many high level names in mining and railway circles attending the meeting, the proposed Tyne Dock was not built for another two decades.

An August 1838 description of a visit to the River Tyne by the British Association for the Advancement of Science gives a vivid image of what the area was like at this time, especially with regards to the riverside terminus of the S&TR:

> The Tyne presented its usual busy, bustling, smoking, steaming aspect, which is perhaps without a parallel on the face of the earth. Father Thames may probably display more wealth afloat and ashore, but I defy him to exhibit scenes of more active, varied, persevering, and successful industry than those which struck our view by land and water during trip from Tynemouth to Newcastle. As crossed the Bar, steam tugs, single and double were buzzing about us in their arduous vocation as thick as bees on a thyme bed.

---

39 *Northern Liberator*, 4 August 1838
40 The National Archives RAIL 1021/87 TE Harrison Sketchbooks
41 *Newcastle Courant*, 19 January 1838
42 *Newcastle Courant*, 6 December 1839

Enginemen at Weatherhill incline *c.* 1910. (Beamish Museum)

The river was alive with craft of all shapes and sizes, and the shores north and south were covered with buildings ... At intervals, along the high banks, the railways from the collieries showed their shipping terminations in platforms surmounting tall piers, beneath which ships receive their cargoes directly into the holds from trap-doors or guiding-shoots above, into which the coal waggons deliver their burdens *tout a coup* ... Beyond, and all around, north and south, new railways are in progress of formation, to our into the ever-gaping mouths of the Shields' colliers additional millions of tonnes to be raised from the distant pits, through both counties of Durham and Northumberland, which, for want of such mechanical accommodation, have not yet been able to bring their products to a profitable marker. At South Shields, the Stanhope and Tyne Railway Company are already in active operation, and the Durham Junction and Brandling Junction Companies are about to open. Everything around is redolent of coal. Air, earth, and water are fulfilled with its manifestations. One hundred and ten steamers are impelled by its power along the red-inky surface of the river. Numberless coke furnaces and chemical factories glow and puff along its banks, each lending a coal-black whiff of its own to the picturesque masses which roll like thunder-clouds along the valley of the river.[43]

The S&TR moved a considerable amount of coal: in 1841, 510,000 tonnes of coal, 22 per cent of the total shipped by the six largest railways in the North East, were shipped by

---

43 *Morning Post*, 22 August 1838 (report dated Monday morning, 19 August)

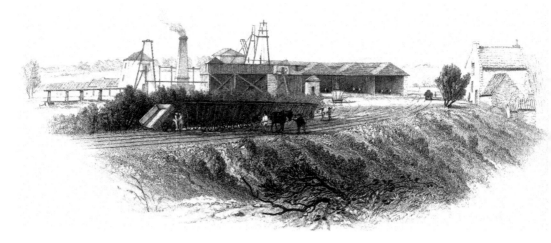

Late 1830s view of Pelton Colliery by Thomas Harrison Hair.

the railway.[44] Evidence given at an inquiry into the Brandling Junction Railway included further impressive statistics regarding the shipping powers of the S&TR at South Shields. When asked how much coal they could ship a day, they responded, 'it has never yet been fully tried what we can do. In one day we have shipped upwards of 100 chaldrons and sometimes 200 at a drop.'[45] As well as having a greater number of drops compared to the Brandling Junction Railway, the S&TR's drops were better sited. The drops were sited at the river where there was more water, and it was possible to lay a tier of ten to twelve ships at a time ready for loading, the Brandling Junction's staithman considering that the S&TR's drops were 'altogether more convenient'. The suitability of the S&TR's drops was such that the men on the S&TR drops did not work on Saturdays, whereas their equivalents on the Brandling Junction had to and, at other times, when required, to avoid the risk of ships lying aground.[46]

An explosion at St Hilda Pit, South Shields, on 28 June 1839 led to subscribers sending donations to support injured victims and the families of those killed. A list published, of subscribers in South Shields, had the S&TR subscribing £21 to the fund, second only in size to the Bishop of Durham's subscription of £31 and 10 shillings, which came 'with a solemn Warning to Use Safety Lamps'.[47] Another charitable act by the company's directors, which with the benefit of hindsight and knowledge of the S&TR financial troubles can seem frivolous, was the presentation of a bell for St Thomas' Church, built 0.5 miles to the north of the line, at Annfield Plain. The church itself opened in July 1841, several months after the S&TR ceased to exist.[48]

44 Tomlinson, W. W., *The North Eastern Railway: Its Rise and Development* (Newcastle: Andrew Reid & Co, 1914), p. 359
45 The National Archives RAIL 64/7
46 The National Archives RAIL 64/7
47 *Newcastle Courant*, 19 July 1839
48 Richardson, M. A., *The Local Historian's Table Book Historical Division Volume V* (Newcastle: MA Richardson, 1846), p. 281–282

View from a modern road bridge down to the end of the S&TR route at South Shields. From here, rails led to the coal drops along the Tyne, just visible behind the trees. The stone walling of the cutting seen to the right is likely original to the opening of the line.

In August 1839 a line was opened between Sacriston Colliery and Waldridge, where the link with the S&TR was made. The opening of this line was done with the usual celebrations. The first train of coal from Sacriston were part of a procession including a band, colliery owners, workmen, and others, travelling with the train to the junction with the S&TR from where the coal moved on to South Shields. When the wagons returned, the workmen of the colliery were given a 'substantial and comfortable' dinner attended by the overmen of the colliery. Later, they were joined by the wives and daughters of the workmen for tea with the festivities ending in a 'merry dance'.[49] The linking of another colliery to the line would have provided welcome additional traffic. In the same year, though, a serious blow was dealt to the traffic on the line with the loss of traffic from Tanfield Moor Colliery, which now went via the Brandling Junction Railway, which was relaying the Tanfield Waggonway with iron rails. The lime traffic from Stanhope was far below expectations. The original plan for the railway forecasted, wildly optimistically, a huge demand for, and subsequent sales of, lime along the line. This did not occur and meant that the substantial amount of money loaned to the S&TR to build the railway could not be repaid. To try and save money, lime making stopped and the line from Stanhope to Carr House was closed in 1839, with the railway focusing

49 Richardson, M. A., *The Local Historian's Table Book Historical Division Volume V* (Newcastle: MA Richardson, 1846), p. 130

Above and below: Original drops used for the landsale of lime and coal at Whitehall, near Rowley, from 1835 onwards. The setting up of lime and coal depots along the line in relatively sparsely populated areas such as here showed the intention of the S&TR to make large profits from landsale of lime and coal, which did not materialise. They still survive in good condition, next to a road, but are often hidden by vegetation.

on the movement of coal. Despite the money made in moving large amounts of coal, even with the loss of the Tanfield Moor traffic, it would need to be substantially higher in order to keep the company going unless there was more investment, which did not occur. The loss of the Tanfield Moor traffic and the cessation of the lime trade marked the beginning of the end, although it was to be another year before the seriousness of the situation became apparent.

The self-acting gravity inclines used by the S&TR were, it was discovered, not significantly cheaper than those requiring stationary steam engines, despite the work being effectively done for free. It was estimated in 1839 that the expenses were £415 per mile for the self-acting inclines, and £485 per mile for stationary engine worked inclines. The ropes in use on the S&TR – sixty in total with a total length of 68 miles – were tarred hemp, which were unlikely to last a year, although, fortunately, the railway closed annually in the month of January when the coal mines that the line served shut down, allowing time for maintenance work on the inclines and rope renewal.

A joining line between the under-construction Brandling Junction Railway and S&TR at Brockley Whins was completed in the summer of 1839, which, via the Durham Junction Railway branching off the S&TR to head over Victoria Viaduct (the construction of which was supervised by T. E. Harrison) and cross the Wear, meant that passengers could be conveyed from Gateshead and other parts of the Brandling Junction to Durham and Stockton. It also allowed coals from the S&TR to be shipped via Wearmouth. The opening of the Victoria Viaduct and viewing of the line in August 1838 involved two passenger trains from South Shields to the viaduct, each train containing around 400 passengers. On the return journey, while crossing the viaduct, the second train ran into the rear carriages of the first train causing serious injuries – this had an effect on T. E. Harrison following the fatalities on the opening of the first half of the S&TR on Weatherhill incline, and he would no longer allow large-scale ceremonies or celebrations on railways he controlled.[50] As the S&TR had half the shares in the Durham Junction Railway, as agreed before it opened, the S&TR provided the locomotives and rolling stock that worked the line. The commencement, in 1840, of a passenger service on the line to Rainton Meadows saw the S&TR stop the service on their line to the Durham turnpike road.

In December 1839 a mine worker by the name of Matthew Willey was walking home to Vigo after work at Ouston pit with his daughter. While walking on the tracks of the railway, he was knocked down by the passenger carriage from South Shields (presumably on the line where it was worked by the Vigo incline engine), the wheel running over his leg and fracturing it. His daughter received severe injuries to her head and other parts of her body. Mr Hudson, a surgeon at nearby Chester-le-Street, attended and amputated Matthew Willey's leg above the knee that evening. Matthew Willey, as a member of the Loyal Mechanics Lodge of Odd Fellows, was awarded an allowance and a present on account of the injuries sustained, and were both reported two weeks later as recovering.[51]

---

50 Hodgson, G. B., *The Borough of South Shields: From the Earliest Period to the Close of the Nineteenth Century* (Newcastle: Andrew Reid & Co., 1903), p. 388

51 *Newcastle Courant*, 27 December 1839

CHAPTER 6

The End of the Stanhope & Tyne Railroad Company

Wright & Co., a banking firm of Covent Garden, London, failed in November 1840. The ending of a small banking firm in London had effects that rippled all the way northward to commence the downfall of the S&TR. The firm had lent money to the S&TR, and, additionally, one of the partners, J. Wright, was a director. The financial confidence creditors of the S&TR had in the railway was ruined. Once word got out about the failure of Wright & Co. and its link to the S&TR – by the end of 1840 the S&TR was £440,000 in debt – the creditors demanded their money for unpaid bills. The Newcastle banks, which had endorsed the S&TR's constant rolling over of unpaid bills, fearing their customers would demand their deposited money and ruin them as a result, refused to continue endorsing the S&TR. A rapid, unavoidable financial catastrophe faced the S&TR. (For more on the financial history of the S&TR, see J. H. Baldwin's 'The Stanhope and Tyne Railway: A Study in Business Failure' in *Early Railways: A Selection of Papers from the First International Railway Conference*, edited by Andy Guy and Jim Rees (London: Newcomen Society, 2001), pp. 325–341)

As a private company without an Act of Parliament or royal charter, shareholders were liable for the failings of the company as well as being able to reap the benefits of success, and could be called upon to pay a company's debts; this is what happened in the case of the S&TR. As he had taken payment for his consultancy of the construction of the line in shares, Robert Stephenson, who like his father had worked so hard for the wealth he had earned, now suddenly faced ruin. The rest of the forty-nine shareholders were also in a dire situation, but Stephenson was particularly vulnerable owing to his wealth and position. Stephenson's solicitor and friend, Charles Parker, provided much needed support and suggested an extraordinary general meeting of the company. This was held on 2 January 1841, and the decision was taken to close the old company and found a new one, this time with an Act of Parliament. In order to do so, owing to the debts of the company (despite its huge assets), many thousands of pounds had to be raised by those interested in keeping the railway running, Stephenson transferring half of his share in Robert Stephenson & Co. to his father.

Original S&TR bridge surviving to the north of Hownes Gill.

The S&TR was dissolved on 5 February 1841.[52] The newly formed Pontop & South Shields Railway (P&SSR), which involved twenty-five of the forty-nine original shareholders of the S&TR, took over the line and its assets, including locomotives that were still in use, and received its Act of Parliament in May 1842, Robert Stephenson becoming its first chairman in August. In the meantime, near the line at Consett, a new works that was to change the fortunes of the closed part of the line came into being. In 1840 the Derwent Iron Works was set up by Jonathan Richardson, choosing Consett as its base owing to the proximity of coal and iron ore. Railways were the only efficient means of moving this in bulk, and additionally the ironmaking process needed limestone as a flux to remove impurities. The P&SSR was not interested in reopening the line from Carr House to the limestone quarries at Crawleyside so sold this section to the Derwent Iron Company, who reopened the line for their use. As far as can be ascertained, the operation of this line continued as it had under the S&TR with a mixture of inclines worked by gravity, stationary engines and horse-worked sections. At one stage it was decided to work the line between Weatherhill and the Parkhead wheel by the Weatherhill incline engine, using a tailrope from the Parkhead wheel to pull the wagons to that point from Weatherhill. At Parkhead, the usual method of tailrope from Meeting Slacks taking them down in that direction was used.

52 Hoole, K., *A Regional History of the Railways of Great Britain Volume 4: The North East* (Newton Abbot: David & Charles, 1965 (1978)), p. 188

While this was more economical in the short term, by reducing the costs of working by horses, it was unsuitable as it put a great strain on the Weatherhill engine.

During this tumultuous period for the line, the railway still proved as dangerous as ever. In order to save the life of a child, one man's rescue attempt led to horrific injury in March 1841. John Briggs, former gamekeeper to the Earl of Durham, saw a child on the P&SSR facing 'impending destruction' from an oncoming train of coal wagons. Although Briggs was able to get the child out the way in time, Briggs caught his foot on the inner side of the rail, fell, and was unable to get clear before the wagons came upon him. The mangling of his leg as the train passed over it meant the leg had to be amputated.[53]

Benjamin Bunn, a bookbinder, was returning home at eight o'clock at night in February 1842 when he crossed the line at Lay Gate Lane, near South Shields, when he was struck by a locomotive pulling a train. The fifty-year-old man was so severely injured he died later that night, leaving a wife and ten children. The inquest returned a verdict of accidental death with a deodand of one shilling placed on the engine of the train. A deodand was a legal term that meant an object could become forfeited or 'given to God' if it had caused a death which was abolished in 1846. What this meant in real terms was that a fine was payable by its owner. A week after Bunn's demise,

Enginemen's cottages at Weatherhill incline. They became designated 'K4' in the S&DR's register of buildings owned by the company, each letter designating the area they were in. (Beamish Museum)

53 Richardson, M. A., *The Local Historian's Table Book Historical Division Volume V* (Newcastle: 1846), p. 247

another death occurred at South Shields when a boy climbed onto a train of wagons on the line but fell off and was run over, dying the next day.[54]

Another accident resulting in a deodand occurred at the Stanhope end of the line, now under operation by the Derwent Iron Company in July 1842. Three wagons loaded with lime were being hauled up the Crawleyside engine when suddenly their progress slowed as the stationary engine ran low on steam. The bankrider and three others with him got off the wagons sensing danger, when suddenly the piece of iron (known as a 'conductor') that the haulage rope was attached to suddenly broke. The three wagons headed down the incline at considerable speed, leaving clouds of lime dust in their wake, and the second and third wagons came off the line. The first wagon continued to a point where the line curved, where the wagon left the line. A public footpath crossed the line here, and upon it were three boys. The wagon flew across the children, bruising the head and face of one child, George Teasdale, and severing the head from the neck of eight-year-old James Kemp. The third boy was almost entirely uninjured. A strict investigation followed, and a verdict of accidental death brought. A deodand of £3 was placed on the wagon, with a further deodand of 5 shillings onto the lime the wagon was carrying.[55, 56]

Workers at Crawleyside incline *c*. 1910. (Beamish Museum)

54 *Newcastle Courant*, Friday 4 March 1842
55 Richardson, M. A., *The Local Historian's Table Book Historical Division Volume V* (Newcastle: MA Richardson, 1846), p. 388–389
56 *The Railway Times*, Volume V, No. 30, 23 July 1842

CHAPTER 7

The Pontop & South Shields Railway

The reliance of the Pontop & South Shields Railway (P&SSR) on the fortunes of the coal trade was evidenced in the half-yearly meeting of the railway, held on Saturday 10 August 1844, declaring that the

> receipts of the past half-year were not so favourable as the directors had in the early part of it reason to anticipate. This was entirely owing to the strike of the pitmen, which had affected all similar undertakings in the north.

Despite this, a dividend was still declared – as stated, the issue was affecting other railways, the Stockton & Darlington Railway also suffering a loss of traffic owing to the strike.[57] The half-yearly meeting in August 1845 showed a considerable increase of coal compared to the situation the previous year. As well as the ending of the strike, the regulation known as the vend, which had been in place for over a century and limited the amount of coal that could be shipped by a colliery, had been lifted. This resulted in a 'considerable reduction in the shipping price of coal', much to the benefit of the P&SSR, but at that time not accompanied by a reduction in tolls for the colliery owners along the line, despite the colliery owners requests.[58]

Part of the S&TR's route became a link in the East Coast Main Line, from London to the Tyne, in the 1840s, with the opening of the Newcastle & Darlington Junction Railway in June 1844, which ran from Darlington via the Durham Junction Railway, then, via the P&SSR and Brandling Junction Railway, reached Gateshead. The P&SSR became part of the Newcastle & Darlington Junction Railway in 1845 (the Durham Junction and Brandling Junction had both been bought by the Newcastle & Darlington the year before), although remained independent until 1847 when it was absorbed by its owner, which had now become the York, Newcastle & Berwick Railway.

On 8 January 1846 a tragic accident occurred at a ballast hill, at South Shields, which had grown over the years from the ballast brought back by otherwise empty (and therefore

---

57 *The Standard*, Monday 12 August 1844
58 *York Herald*, Saturday 30 August 1845

Eden Colliery, Leadgate. Opening in 1844, this was one of the many collieries that used the P&SSR. Later it was taken over by the Consett Iron Works to supply coal for the furnaces. (Beamish Museum)

unsafe, as they would ride high in the water) sailing colliers returning from London and elsewhere. Temporary rails had been laid from the Newcastle & Darlington Junction Railway's Shields branch, and labourers of the Pontop & South Shields Railway were loading a train of ballast trucks with the material, which mainly consisted of dry gravel with some clay for use on the railway. There was a slight slope to the ballast hill, and this rose to around 40 feet above the level of the temporary rails, the men standing on the slope throwing the ballast into the wagons. As they did so, they undermined the ballast, making it unstable. Suddenly the loose ground gave way, burying three men completely, several others partially, and completely filling the gap between the slope and the wagons, some of which were also buried. One man who was stood high up was carried by the landslide completely over the wagons and deposited on the ground having come to no harm. After the initial shock, those uninjured set to work rescuing those buried. Most were pulled out alive, around a dozen avoiding a grim fate, but two bodies were later found crushed by the ballast up against the wagons. Another man had his thigh bone broken and, at the time of the report, was not expected to live.[59]

On the Sunday evening of 9 October 1849, an accident occurred at a watering station by the River Don, near West Boldon. As a passenger train passed Washington signal station,

59 *Morning Post*, Saturday 10 January 1846

the men observed that as the cabin had closed this must mean the signalman had gone home after the mail train to London had passed. The engine crew would no doubt have been surprised that while stopped at the watering station the mail train came upon them and crashed into the carriage containing workmen, most of whom were asleep before the collision. Three of them were killed and several injured.

In February 1851, George Hardy started work at the engine shops of the York, Newcastle & Berwick Railway at South Shields. The S&TR's tradition of being over engineered, including the locomotives, appears to have continued. Hardy mentions how he was surprised at the superiority of the parts and the precautions made to keep parts together: 'everything was secured by double nuts and a pin to secure them, in fact I found there was as much trouble to prevent parts coming out as there was to make them altogether.'[60]

The Pontop & South Shields branch of the York, Newcastle & Berwick Railway suffered a terrible accident to a new locomotive built for working the Pelton Level,[61] No. 119, on the afternoon of 12 July 1851. At around 1.30 p.m., No. 119, carrying six men, was travelling tender-first along Eden Hill embankment when a rail came out of its chair, the tender leaping off the line, pulling the locomotive with it and sending

Bridge crossing the River Don at Brockley Whins, just to the south of the Pontop Crossing where the Brandling Junction was crossed on the level. The decking is clearly later, but the bridge abutments appear to be original S&TR stonework and thus is likely to have originally supported a wooden deck.

60 Autobiography of George Hardy, p. 19
61 Ibid, p. 20

it rolling over three times as it fell down the 12-foot-high embankment. Two men, fireman Francis Misk and railway inspector John Swinburne, jumped off, but four were trapped underneath the 8-tonne engine when it came to rest. Owing to the weight of the locomotive, despite the efforts of the rescuers, it was some time before those underneath could be extracted. Two were crushed to death – driver John Mann and bankrider William Richardson – with the other two, John Moffatt and John White, suffering broken thighs. At the inquest the line was described as in 'good working condition' by Swinburne, and, similarly, Misk and John Thoburn, overman at Twizell Colliery who attended the scene of the accident, gave testimony to the good condition of the railway, resulting in a verdict of accidental death.[62]

The workshops at South Shields ceased to make locomotives from 1852 when the manager was sent to York.[63] The workshops continued in use to repair locomotives and as a base for repairing the stationary engines on the inclined planes. George Hardy was involved in removing the old engine on the west side of Vigo in the early 1850s, it being replaced by a new diagonal engine placed on the east side of Vigo incline.[64] To safely take locomotives over the inclines and to avoid removing the sheaves that sat between the rails for guiding the incline ropes, the Pontop & South Shields had a practice of fitting extra-long axle boxes to the front wheels to lift up the engine so it would ride clear of the sheaves.[65] Locomotive working between the inclines on the levels continued, with an engine shed being authorised, in 1893, to be built at Pelton Level to replace a 'dilapidated' shed already in existence there.

The existing facilities for shipping coal via the former S&TR and Brandling Junction Railway drops at South Shields had long been known to be inadequate. The creation of the North Eastern Railway (NER) in 1854, by amalgamating the York, Newcastle & Berwick Railway, the York & North Midland Railway and the Leeds Northern Railway, created a huge railway with serious financial clout to be able to build the necessary facilities for moving minerals from the North East to market. Soon after the formation of the NER, work planning started, which began in late 1855 and took just over three years. The Admiralty was strongly against the building of Tyne Dock, as it believed the enclosure of such a large portion of Jarrow Slake would have major changes on the course of the river, and attempted to have the bill thrown out when on its third reading in the House of Commons. After failing to do this, it appealed to the House of Lords.[66]

A grim discovery was made by the contractors building Tyne Dock in March 1856 when the iron framework of a gibbet was discovered, which had lain there for over twenty years. A gibbet consisted of an iron cage, hanging from a tall wooden post, in which the body of an executed prisoner was put on public display after hanging. In 1832, miner William Jobling of South Shields was hanged following the murder of local

---

62 *Newcastle Courant*, Friday 18 July 1851

63 Autobiography of George Hardy, p. 20

64 Ibid, p. 21

65 Ibid, p. 22

66 Hodgson, G. B., *The Borough of South Shields: From the Earliest Period to the Close of the Nineteenth Century* (Newcastle: Andrew Reid & Co., 1903), p. 211

Tyne Dock in the 1890s. (Beamish Museum)

senior magistrate Nicholas Fairles by Jobling's friend – the perpetrator had escaped but Jobling was sentenced as his accomplice and because he did not intervene in the assault which lead to the man's death. After being hung, Jobling was gibbeted at the site of the murder – his body covered in tar to preserve it – before being placed in the iron cage. Jobling's friends removed his body one night soon after he was gibbeted and, after having to initially bury him in the mud of Jarrow Slake to avoid detection, returned the following day, removed the body and gave Jobling a proper burial. After the removal of the gibbet by the contractors it ended up in the hands of Thomas Scott, the staithe master at Tyne Dock. The highly unusual distinction of the North Eastern Railway being the owner of a gibbet cage with a grisly past came to an end in 1887 when it was formally handed over to the Newcastle Society of Antiquaries. It can now be seen on display at South Shields Museum.[67]

In June 1856 the NER made an agreement with Lord Durham to acquire additional land to allow the stationary engine at Vigo, which worked two inclines for a length of nearly 2 miles, to be removed and locomotive working used on this part of the line. This resulted in an additional running line being laid to the north of the existing line. Additionally, the junction with the Beamish Waggonway was moved from the east side of the Great North

67 Hodgson, G. B., *The Borough of South Shields: From the Earliest Period to the Close of the Nineteenth Century* (Newcastle: Andrew Reid & Co., 1903), pp. 375–377

Coal staiths at Tyne Dock *c.* 1910. (Beamish Museum)

Road to the west side. A wooden bridge built over the road replaced the level crossing in 1857 (this was replaced by an iron bridge in 1893, which still stands). Owing to these improvements, locomotives were able to work between Stella Gill and South Shields by 1857.

In the year 1858, 1.2 million tonnes of coal were shipped at South Shields by the North Eastern Railway, 29 per cent of the total amount of coal shipped on the Tyne. The opening of Tyne Dock in March 1859 and its huge shipping capacity, which could and was extended, had an enormous impact on the amount of coal that could be shipped from the North East. The sudden dwarfing of other coal shipping facilities aided the S&DR's entering into a pact with the NER which would result in the mighty S&D, still fiercely independent, eventually becoming a part of the NER in 1863 (although retaining its independence by having its own committee for over a decade). An engine shed was built at Tyne Dock from late 1861, likely opening in 1862, and was home to the locomotives used for hauling wagons between the collieries and Tyne Dock.

CHAPTER 8

Stockton & Darlington Railway Heads North

The Stockton & Darlington Railway (S&DR), which was using coal drops at Middlesbrough as the main outlet for coal by the 1840s, had its main works at Shildon, where the locomotive-worked section of the line originated in the west (with branches worked by inclines and horses stretching further west) and was starting to extend to the north-west. The Prince of Wales Tunnel, which ran for 7/8 of a mile under the town of Shildon, opened in 1842, enabling the line to run towards Bishop Auckland and further into Weardale. The line was initially extended to Crook, and discussions started between the S&DR and the Derwent Iron Works with regards to extending the line to meet the original S&TR line, meaning the products of the ironworks could be shipped by the S&DR. The S&DR, by this point very powerful with a sizeable locomotive fleet and nearly twenty years' experience in moving heavy goods trains, were a suitable choice to move the heavy, bulky goods from the ironworks. The line was surveyed and planned to join the existing railway at the head of Nanny Mayer's incline with an incline at Sunnyside on the climb out from Crook. The line was built through 1844 and was ready by early 1845. Facilities were of course needed to run the railway, and at the meeting point of the two railways these were constructed at Waskerley.

The S&DR and the Derwent Iron Company were in agreement that the S&DR should take over the line from Stanhope to Carr House, including the quarries along it, for sixty years at a payment of £3,000 per annum – as long as the Derwent Iron Company was responsible for providing a large amount of traffic. The rent of £3,000 was based on a valuation of £2,000 for the stationary engines on the line and £1,000 in rent to the owners of the railway and the extensive kilns, quarries and sundry wayleaves along it. The S&DR took over the line from the quarries and kilns at Stanhope to Carr House on 1 January 1845, actually leasing the line (including the route north of Crook to Waskerley) purchased not long after this by a number of S&DR directors forming the Wear & Derwent Junction Railway, which also included the Weardale Extension Railway from Crook to Waskerley. The 23 miles of railway thus added to the Stockton & Darlington Railway and fortunately soon proved a wise investment – it was reported just eight months after the takeover that

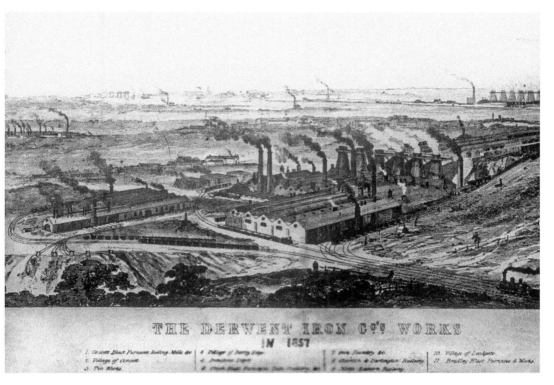

THE DERWENT IRON C.º'S WORKS
IN 1857

Derwent Iron Works at Consett in 1857. (Beamish Museum)

traffic was 'many fold what was originally anticipated' and rising.[68] The use of other names to build and take over new lines was a shrewd move by the S&DR, and in 1846 another of the S&DR's 'children', the Wear Valley Railway, took over the Wear & Derwent Junction Railway, including the Weardale Extension Railway, the Shildon Tunnel Company and the Bishop Auckland & Weardale Railway, which ran from Shildon to Crook. The Act of Parliament for this amalgamation, using a part of the 1845 Wear Valley Act that included provision for the S&DR to take over the line on a 999-year lease, received its royal assent on 22 July 1847 and led to the full takeover of the Wear Valley Railway by the S&DR on 1 October 1847.

The S&DR didn't take long to introduce locomotive working to the route, replacing inclines and horse-worked sections where possible, while also creating and improving goods depots along the line to supplement those built by the S&TR. Part of the original S&TR route between Parkhead and Meeting Slacks was cut-off by building a large embankment to make it better suitable for locomotive working. Another part was levelled off by making the 'Frosterley Cut', a cutting near the site of Meeting Slacks engine house that is still clearly distinguishable (together with the embankment towards Parkhead). It features a large wall on the northern side of the line comprising of old stone sleepers running the majority of the length of the cutting, with a shorter wall made of wooden sleepers. This was to try and prevent snow drifts blocking the cut, but

68 Durham County Records Office D/XD 35/12 Stockton & Darlington Railway AGM 1844–45

it is not known when it was constructed – it is likely to be from the line's operational history at around the time the stone sleepers were replaced with wooden ones. A similar but shorter wall made of stone sleepers exists to the east of Waskerley engine shed before Burnhill Junction.

The creation of a railway centre at Waskerley required an engine shed, and in October 1845 construction was authorised for a shed to fit four engines with tenders.[69] A wagon repair shop was also opened in 1845. Waskerley grew to become a sizeable community, including two churches, two rows of houses and a school with the staff paid for by the S&DR and by succeeding railway companies.

The lack of fences on the line above Waskerley led to the creation of one of the distinguishing features of the route. Many stone boundary markers were placed on both sides of the line from Waskerley onwards and inscribed with S&DR facing the line itself. These still survive in great quantities on the line itself, some toppled over, some nearly buried – and no doubt some actually buried and undetectable – some standing proud with the ground around them worn away, some at jaunty angles, but all of them fascinating witnesses to over 100 years of operation. No doubt for all those that survive, many more were destroyed. Some have also been preserved in museums.

Waskerley engine shed, showing the coaling stage on the left and another part of the engine shed in the background. The first shed was built here in 1845, the second in 1856. (Head of Steam – Darlington Railway Museum)

69 Hoole, K., *North Eastern Locomotive Sheds* (Newton Abbot: David & Charles, 1972), p. 74

Stockton & Darlington Railway Tory Class locomotive No. 25, *Derwent*, built by A. Kitching of Darlington in 1845. *Derwent* was one of the Tory Class locomotives based at Waskerley and was later involved in the construction of nearby Smiddy Shaw Reservoir in the 1870s. It can now be seen on display at Head of Steam – Darlington Railway Museum.

The incline at Hownes Gill had long been a serious bar to the movement of traffic towards Consett by the S&DR. At some point, prior to 1853, the cradles had been dispensed with and wagons were instead run three at a time down and up the incline. This was, however, far from ideal as it often caused wagonloads, such as finished goods like rails from the ironworks, to fall off! There was no other option but to take up the costly option of building a viaduct.

In 1856, Thomas Bouch (better known for his Tay Bridge, which infamously collapsed in 1879) had his plan approved for a bridge over Hownes Gill, the first brick being laid in February 1857. As construction continued on the viaduct, the needs of the ironworks at Consett were growing. By August 1857 the ironworks were using ninety wagons of limestone (at 3 tonnes per wagon) daily, requesting a delivery of 110 wagons a day until further notice to ensure supplies were available.[70]

The viaduct opened for use on Friday 25 June 1858. The directors of the S&DR held a board meeting at the viaduct that day featuring the usual method of testing a new bridge – by placing a load as heavy as possible on it:

> At half-past twelve a train of 72 laden waggons was passed slowly over the bridge without the slightest signs of shake or deflection being observable. Afterwards a locomotive,

70 The National Archives RAIL 667/59

Stockton & Darlington Railway boundary marker between Parkhead and Meeting Slacks.

appropriately termed "The Leader," repeated this experiment, and then the party, with numbers of workmen, passed and repassed along the entire length at a quick pace, and, ultimately, a heavily laden coach train, with a full complement, satisfactorily proved the perfection of the work, which, during its progress, has been unattended by any accident, and on its completion has been opened with complete success.[71]

With the opening of Hownes Gill Viaduct, the incline at Carr House was closed and used by locomotives. Work to avoid Nanny Mayer's incline was underway, and in July 1859 the Burnhill deviation opened. From Whitehall, west of Rowley, the line split from the original S&TR route and gained height to Burnhill, where trains could continue to Tow Law and onward to Crook or Bishop Auckland (as passenger trains now did). If they were using the Waskerley line they would have to reverse onto the S&DR route to Waskerley from the Tow Law direction. Waskerley remained as a goods station but a small passenger station was built at Burnhill, accessible only via a footpath, for those travelling to or from Waskerley.

Side view of Hownes Gill Viaduct showing a North Eastern Railway Fletcher 901 Class 2-4-0 locomotive pulling a short passenger train including a horsebox. (Beamish Museum)

71 *Newcastle Courant*, Friday 2 July 1858

CHAPTER 9

North Eastern Railway

The 1860s were to see the two halves of the S&TR route operated by the same company for the first time in over twenty years. In 1863 the Stockton & Darlington Railway became part of the North Eastern Railway. The fierce independence of the S&DR was shown in that it was run by a separate committee within the NER for over ten years and still showed its individual identity until then. The two parts of the line comprising the Waskerley branch and the Pontop & South Shields branch would continue to be operated separately.

Under the NER's Darlington section – effectively the continued S&DR in all but name – the line between Rowley ('Cold' was officially dropped from its name in 1868, although

Rowley station looking west *c.* 1914. (Beamish Museum)

Replacement cylinder on the Weatherhill engine.

the name Cold Rowley unofficially stayed for years after) and Hownes Gill was doubled to increase traffic. In 1873 the decision was made to build a more substantial station, with the Darlington section asking architect William Peachey to plan for a 'very small station'. The impressive stone-built station featured three arches supported by two 'barley twist' iron columns in the open central waiting area, which was arranged so that the station received the maximum benefit of the sun as it rose and set in the day. It also had an enclosed waiting area for female travellers. Rowley station was to be the first building moved onto the Beamish open-air museum site, completed by 1975. The rebuilding of the station at Rowley is quite remarkable – not only was it the first building of many to be relocated to Beamish, but its setting at Beamish is exactly how it was at Rowley. The signalbox (albeit from Carr House West, just west of Consett and also on the S&TR route) is in the same position as the 1914 signalbox was at Rowley. The footbridge that leads from the recreated 1913 town is in the same position, relative to the station, as the road bridge, which carries the A68, was at Rowley.

After the conversion of much of the original S&TR line to locomotive working, by the 1880s just three stationary engine worked inclines remained – Crawleyside, Weatherhill and Loud Bank. The original engine at Crawleyside was replaced with a marine type in the 1860s, giving it increased capacity. The original 1833-built cylinder of the Weatherhill burst in the 1880s, doing 'considerable damage'. Fortunately, a spare was available. The Tanfield branch, which had been converted to iron rails and included several stationary engines, following its takeover by the Brandling Junction Railway in the late 1830s and early 1840s, had its engine-worked incline sections converted to locomotive working in 1881. The now redundant cylinder from the Bowes Bridge stationary engine was fitted to the Weatherhill incline as a replacement, which it continued with until closure.

To further allow locomotive working on the line towards Consett, in 1886 a deviation opened at Annfield Plain to bypass the Loud Bank incline. A much longer deviation would be required to bypass the remaining inclines, a 6.5-mile deviation being constructed, leaving the original route at South Pelaw and going via Beamish, running to the north of the original route. Opening to mineral traffic in 1893, it still featured many steep gradients, which required very hard work from the locomotives heading west towards Consett. Although the deviation was done with the transport of minerals in mind, it also allowed a passenger and goods service to be provided. After completion of the necessary stations and other work this was opened in 1894. A service ran from Newcastle via Bensham and Birtley, diverging from the East Coast Main Line at Ouston Junction. Then onwards it followed the deviated S&TR route to the new stations at Pelton, Beamish, Shieldrow (or Shield Row – later renamed West Stanley), Annfield Plain, Ladgate, Consett and then on to Blackhill where the service terminated. Other services could also be joined: north towards Newcastle, via Shotley Bridge and Rowlands Gill; south-east towards Durham, via Lanchester; or south, via Rowley, towards Bishop Auckland and Darlington. Despite the opening of the deviation, the inclines on the original route were to remain in use for over fifty years.

The NER equipped itself with a large fleet of snowploughs, eventually totalling twenty-four. In 1895 Waskerley engine shed had North Eastern Railway wooden snowplough No. 5, built to diagram U29 in November 1888. Snowplough No. 5 was built

London & North Eastern Railway V1 Class 2-6-2T passenger locomotive No. 446 at Consett station (photo taken from the window of No. 2 Station Terrace) in June 1935, when the locomotive was just two months old. It was a typical example of the large tank engines used by the LNER on passenger services on the deviated Stanhope & Tyne route. (Beamish Museum)

on a six-wheel chassis on a 12-foot-long underframe and was 26 feet 9.5 inches from the front tip of the plough to the dumb buffers on the rear. 11-feet 2 inches high, there was space for a crew compartment for the men who would get out and stand clear while the snowplough was rammed into the snow, then go to work to clear the dislocated snow off the line by shovel. The inside was fitted with heating together with a cooking stove and a coal and firewood bunker to fuel it. In July 1901 snowplough No. 14 was built joining No. 5 at Waskerley. Where possible, snowploughs operated in pairs, one facing each way with the locomotives sandwiched in-between in case, while heading one way, snow made a return journey difficult. No. 5 and No. 14 were allocated to Waskerley until at least 1935 and snowploughs No. 18 and No. 20 were photographed in this decade. There was certainly plenty of work for them. A notable occurrence in the winter of 1937 saw two snowploughs and three locomotives come off the line at Weatherhill while clearing deep drifts of snow. It was common in both world wars for prisoners of war held in the area to assist in clearing the snow off the railway lines. The snowploughs were removed with the closure of Waskerley shed. At some point in its history, a wall of sleepers was built near the incline head at Weatherhill in order to try and reduce the risk of drifts blocking the line. Much of the wall remains.[72] Despite the presence of snowploughs,

---

72 Williamson, D., & Williamson, C., *Railway Snowploughs in the North East* (North Eastern Railway Association, 2014)

they were not a guarantee the lines could remain open and in 1910, owing to a derailed snowplough, a passenger train was stuck at Rowley for several days.

In the 1910s there were around 100,000 tonnes of limestone a year being transported from the kilns north of Stanhope, via the old Stanhope & Tyne line, mostly going to Consett for the iron and steel works. At the same time, traffic going down the inclines totalled around 1,000 tonnes of coal and coke annually.[73] Consett had a population of around 11,000 by the 1910s. The eight blast furnaces needed 550,000 tonnes of iron ore per annum and gave an output of 250,000 tonnes of iron and steel.[74] When it is considered that all these products were moved in and out of Consett by rail, the importance of the Stanhope & Tyne route – as well as other lines serving the area – is clear.

By 1912 over 5 million tonnes of coal was transiting through Stella Gill annually, with 4 million being for shipment. 85 per cent of the 4 million travelled through Tyne Dock, via Washington, and the remaining 15 per cent through Dunston Staiths, via Ouston Junction and Low Fell. The remaining amount was landsale, mainly large factories and gasworks.[75] By this point, Tyne Dock was the largest coal shipping point in the North East with shipments of over 7 million tonnes from around 250 different collieries.[76]

Two NER snowploughs at South Pelaw Junction. (Beamish Museum)

73 *NER Magazine*, July 1919, p. 133
74 Trade and Commerce of the NER District 1912, p. 72
75 Trade and Commerce of the NER District, 1912, p. 18
76 Trade and Commerce of the NER District 1912, p. 19

1896 view of Waldridge Colliery showing NER P4 10.5-tonne hopper wagons. (Beamish Museum)

Loaded NER P4 10.5-tonne hopper at Stella Gill, in 1900, with a group photograph of shunters. (Beamish Museum)

View of Morrison Pit, Annfield Plain (later Morrison Busty), *c.* 1916. From left to right there are examples of P6 15-tonne hoppers, P4 10.5-tonne hoppers and P7 20-tonne hoppers. (Beamish Museum)

The peak year for the NER, 1913, saw the company handle 44,165,950 tonnes of coal and coke (excluding that for railway use), and 2,954,300 tonnes of lime and limestone.[77] The majority of limestone came from County Durham, which, in 1913, accounted for 2.26 million tonnes of limestone – the total output of limestone in the United Kingdom and Isle of Man was 12.74 million tonnes in that year.[78]

The First World War and its insatiable demand for iron and steel placed further strain on the line as Consett was busier than ever, which led to fears that the 1833 stationary engine at Weatherhill would break or otherwise be unable to cope with the increased demand placed on it. A new engine was built, which also required a new winding house, but was not operational until 1919. New quarries opened to cater for the demand for limestone. The impact of the war on food supply led to various initiatives being taken by Britain's railways – the Great Central Railway had the novel 'poultry train' which demonstrated the benefits of keeping chickens. The North Eastern Railway loaned this for a while in 1917 and visited various NER locations, including Tyne Dock on Monday 23 April 1917 and Consett on Saturday 12 May 1917 (which coincided with Consett's market day).[79]

The new incline engine at Weatherhill was of great contrast to the 1833 original. The following information and drawing given in the *North Eastern Railway Magazine* of July 1919 describes the new machinery:

---

77 NER Mineral Statistics 1854–1913, pp. 3–4
78 NER Mineral Statistics 1854–1913, p. 82
79 *NER Magazine*, April 1917, p. 73

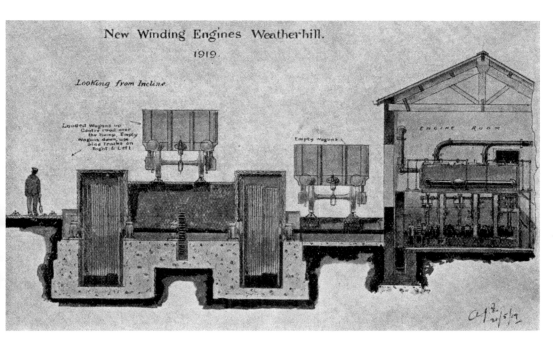

New Winding Engines Weatherhill.

1919.

Looking from Incline

Loaded Wagons up Centre road over the Hump. Empty Wagons down, use Side Tracks on Right & Left.

Empty Wagons

ENGINE ROOM

The 1919 Weatherhill incline engine.

In the new machinery, a sketch of which is also given, readers will recognise the marine type of engine (the shaft revolving a spur wheel instead of a propeller). There are one high and two low pressure cylinders of 18 in., 21 in., and 21 in. stroke respectively with all the fittings usual on this class of engine. The engineman (who, by the way, is the same man as had attended the old engine during its last 25 years of service), has no longer to work a troublesome ' gab' gear, the reversal of the engine being now, of course, done by gear on the engine under the control of a single lever. The brake is on the fly wheel as with the old engine, and emergency brakes are provided on each drum. The drums, on each of which over a mile of rope is coiled, are very similar to those used in the old arrangement, but it will be noticed that whereas they were previously placed aloft, they are now on the ground line.

The old drums were raised high to suit the contour of the incline, there being a ' bank head' to clear, but the engineer of to-day thinks nothing of removing a few hundred tonnes of rock, and this was done in the present instance, the country being made (as far as possible) to suit the engines instead of, as with our forefathers, the engines to suit the country.

It should be explained that an artificial hump is provided at the top of the incline, so that when the two or three wagons which form a trip are unhooked after their journey they travel some distance by gravitation and clear of the bank head, eventually forming a train which is taken forward by an ordinary locomotive. The position of the wagons seen in the sketch of new station show a wagon on this hump which also forms the housing for the drums.

The government control of most of Britain's railways during the First World War remained after the end of the war and saw the creation of the 'Big Four' in the Transport Act of 1921,

Artists view of Crawleyside and Weatherhill inclines, seen from the adjacent road.

Limestone quarries at Stanhope, seen in 1924.

Commemorative train of P7 20-tonne hopper wagons, in 1934, at Waldridge Bank Foot to mark the centenary of the S&TR.

which, in 1923, saw the North Eastern Railway become part of the London & North Eastern Railway (LNER). As a result of the creation of the LNER, as of 1 July 1923, Parkhead goods station was renamed to Blanchland, a quaint village just over 6 miles from Parkhead itself. This was done to avoid confusion with the ex-North British Railway Parkhead station in Glasgow. Misconsigned goods for Glasgow could end up on the desolate moors, high above Stanhope, and would not be likely to amuse the consignee or consignor! The goods stations at Waskerley and Parkhead/Blanchland would play an important role in serving the needs of a widespread community across the area. Parkhead was one of nine stations in the North Eastern Area of the London & North Eastern Railway to have its name changed to avoid duplication.[80]

The centenary of the S&TR was marked on 10 September 1934 at Waldridge Bank Foot. Not on the same scale as the Stockton & Darlington centenary celebrations of 1925 but impressive nonetheless, the event included retired workers from the inclines and various dignitaries, as well as a large crowd of sightseers present when Sir Wilson, a director of the LNER, gave the signal to run a set of wagons up and down the incline. The occasion warranted a 20-tonne hopper wagon specially decorated for the occasion, which was almost certainly the only time this ever happened! Sir Wilson unveiled a tablet at Pelton Fell that states, 'This tablet was erected on 10 Sept 1934 to commemorate the centenary of the opening of the Stanhope and Tyne Railway operated partly by self acting inclines'. The tablet, happily, still exists in the collection at Head of Steam, Darlington Railway Museum. As a reminder of the day, a chromium plated model of the 'lock chain', used for attaching ropes to wagons, was made by the staff at the Signal & Telegraph Shops at York and presented to Sir Wilson by a Mr W. Curry, formerly a brakesman on the inclines for fifty-six years.

80 *NER Magazine*, September 1923, p. 240

CHAPTER 10

Decline and Closures

In May 1939 the passenger service was withdrawn between Tow Law and Blackhill, with Burnhill and Rowley stations closing for passengers. As Burnhill had no goods service it was closed but Rowley stayed open for goods. The Second World War saw the line severed, just south of Burnhill Junction, by the construction of Saltersgate Ammunition Depot, which was used to store ammunition produced at Newton Aycliffe Royal Ordnance Factory. The ammunition depot was served by rail, which had a transfer siding and a narrow-gauge railway for moving the ammunition around the site. The ammunition depot meant that the Waskerley branch's link to the south was also cut-off, and now all, even southbound, trains coming from Waskerley had to reverse at Burnhill Junction to head north towards Consett (and vice versa for trains going to Waskerley). The passenger service to Crook and Tow Law now had to be served by engines based at Darlington, and the reduced need for the engine shed at Waskerley saw it closing in 1940 and the engines left transferring to Consett. This was the beginning of the end for Waskerley as a village.

The continued use of the self-acting gravity inclines along the Pontop & South Shields branch, taking coal wagons from collieries in the Annfield Plain area to Stella

North Eastern Railway
N10 Class 0-6-2T
locomotive No. 69093
at Pelton Fell in
British Railways days.
(Beamish Museum)

Gill (from where they were marshalled and taken to Dunston, Tyne Dock or Sunderland South Dock, despite the existence of locomotive-worked deviations), was also proving an unnecessary additional expenditure by the late 1930s. In July 1939 it was outlined how the three inclines at Waldridge, Eden Hill and Stanley were expensive to work. Although it was using the heavy loaded wagons descending the inclines to pull the lighter empty wagons uphill, it still required locomotives to work the levels in-between the inclines and shunt the wagons at either end. There was also expenditure in the wages of men employed to work the inclines and maintenance costs, etc. It was proposed to close Eden Hill and Stanley inclines, which were working sixteen hours a day, and reduce the working at Waldridge incline (which had to stay open as it was the only way of serving the colliery at the head of the incline) to eight hours a day. This would save nearly £5,000 a year, considering the saving of over £7,000 by closing them was offset by the additional cost of working the traffic by locomotives over the deviation route, including improvements to signalling and telephone facilities. The Second World War meant that the recommendations were not followed through until shortly after the end of the war.

The resulting reorganisation led, at the same time, to a proposal to close the engine sheds at Annfield Plain and Waskerley, focusing the locomotives at Consett engine shed. In July 1939 there were four engines at Consett, five at Waskerley and six at Annfield Plain, and by concentrating the locomotives in the area at Consett the need for engines would be reduced from fifteen to thirteen. The original engine shed at Consett was too

Consett shed, seen in the British Railways era, was mainly home to NER Q6 Class 0-8-0 heavy goods locomotives. (Beamish Museum)

small, so to increase the undercover space available, a similar brick-built engine shed was built alongside the original.[81] The engine sheds at Waskerley and Annfield Plain both closed in September 1940, with the locomotives focusing on Consett as planned, although at least one of the J25 locomotives from Annfield Plain was among the forty J25s sent to the Great Western Railway for the duration of the war to replace their 'Dean Goods' locomotives requisitioned by the War Department. This was to be the beginning of the end of the remarkable community at Waskerley. By the 1960s a goods agent remained at Waskerley for the movement of sand from the quarries around Weatherhill and Blanchland with a goods train powered by a Q6 locomotive running two or three times a week.

Declining traffic and the need for rationalisation by the newly formed (on 1 January 1948) British Railways (BR) on the Waskerley branch meant the end was near for the last two stationary engines on the line. In 1949, the lime depots at Crawleyside delivered 3,182 tonnes of clotted lime from the kilns to a road haulier, who mainly just took it 100 yards down the road to a crushing plant, earning £451 for British Railways. This traffic was due to end soon, owing to an agreement to replace the rails with a roadway to take the lime directly from the kilns to the crusher by lorry. A further 10,474 tonnes of clotted lime were moved up the inclines, and 144 tonnes of coal received to be held in reserve at the depots, but the majority was now being delivered by road from Consett. Ground lime and

One of the last – if not the last – trains to pass through Waskerley was English Electric 350 hp Class 08 diesel locomotive D3875, passing the old station house in 1967. (Beamish Museum)

---

81 TNA RAIL 390/1832

Above and below: Iron ore trains on the line powered by British Railways Standard 9F Class 2-10-0 heavy goods locomotives. (Beamish Museum)

limestone had ceased to travel via the inclines. It was transported by covered vans that could not fit through Hog Hill Tunnel, so instead was taken by lorry to Stanhope station and loaded there. By 1950, on average, just two sets of wagons were using the inclines each day, and in November 1950 the decision was made to close the Weatherhill and Crawley inclines and the line at Crawleyside served by the inclines. After expenditure of £1,100 to improve the loading dock at Stanhope station, on the Wear Valley line that was still open to provide an alternative service for traders, it was estimated that closing the inclines would save BR £4,431 a year.[82]

The ironore trains from Tyne Dock to Consett became a well-known feature of the line in the BR era that have been well covered in magazine articles and books during and since then. The gradient going up towards Consett, even on the deviations, made for heavy going even for the large locomotives employed, including some of the most powerful ever seen on Britain's railways, such as the British Railways Standard 9F 2-10-0s. The weight of the trains, plus the gradients, meant that two locomotives were often used, one at the front pulling the train and the other at the rear, banking to assist it up the slopes.

Although the British Railways Standard locomotives were built with a life of fifty years or so, the rapid modernisation of British Railways, together with reducing traffic, meant Consett shed closed in 1965 and the remaining trains of iron ore to Consett were moved by Type 2 (later known as Class 24) diesel locomotive. In 1955 passenger services had been removed along the line from Pelton to Consett, owing to low passenger numbers – goods services remained for a few years longer, Beamish and West Stanley losing theirs in 1960 and 1961 respectively, Annfield Plain and Leadgate retaining theirs until 1964. April 1968 saw the end of the Waskerley branch as it was uneconomical to continue running. Road transport took over from rail. The goods stations at Waskerley and Blanchland closed in August 1965 and Rowley goods station lasted until June 1966, but this did not see the end of trains running on the line. An English Electric Type 3 diesel electric locomotive (later known as a Class 37), with brake tender, was seen collecting 13-tonne mineral wagons from the various sidings along the branch Weatherhill and Blanchland on 26 October 1965.[83] An English Electric 350 hp (later known a Class 08) diesel locomotive was photographed on a goods train at Waskerley having come down the line from Meeting Slacks on 14 February 1967. The closure of the line from Weatherhill and to Burnhill Junction came in April 1968. The remaining section of the Waskerley branch from Burnhill to Consett closed in May 1969.

Aside from iron ore traffic, coal was still moving along the line, but collieries were starting to close. The last incline, Waldridge, closed in 1969 after Craghead Colliery, the last of the pits that used the once crowded marshalling yard at Stella Gill, closed. More closures occurred on the original route of the line, with the route south of Brockley Whins, through Boldon and Washington, closing in 1967 together with the shed at Tyne Dock. Iron ore trains to Consett now had to proceed a more circuitous route via the East Coast Main Line. The crossing at Brockley Whins, known as Pontop crossing for many years, was kept in use until the 1980s as the National Coal Board took over

---

82 TNA AN 13/1715 Closure of Weatherhill and Crawley inclines, NER
83 Stobbs, A. W., *Memories of the LNER South-west Durham* (A. W. Stobbs, 1989), pp. 39–40

NER Q7 Class 0-8-0 heavy goods locomotive No. 63467 at Annfield Plain station, now the site of a Tesco supermarket. In the background is the Annfield Plain Co-op, part of which has been rebuilt at Beamish Museum. The school to the right of the relocated Co-op still stands. (Beamish Museum)

a short section of line so that it could serve Boldon Colliery, which closed in 1982. The 1834 S&TR coal and lime depot at West Boldon was still standing when the line closed. By the time Frank Atkinson, the founder of Beamish Museum, was looking for suitable buildings it was the only building left of West Boldon station and used by a farmer to store agricultural equipment. Frank Atkinson was able to convince British Railways to leave the depot in place until such a time as his planned open-air museum was a reality and able to take it. When British Railways informed Frank that the building had to go, the Friends of Beamish were able to take it down and start to re-erect it on the recreated Rowley station site. To give a suitable sense of scale for the site at Rowley, which was meant to be a small country station, four of the six bays of the depots were rebuilt at Beamish.[84]

In the 1970s the line from South Pelaw continued in use but the Class 24s were replaced with Class 37 diesels. The iron ore came up from Redcar iron ore terminal from 1974 using new 100-tonne tippler wagons, which replaced the distinctive 56-tonne wagons. The

---

84 Atkinson, F., *The Man Who Made Beamish: An Autobiography* (Gateshead: Northern Books, 1999), pp. 120–121

August 1969 and new traffic for the line. Seen here is a train pulled by two Class 37 diesel locomotives hauling Torpedo wagons, which contained molten iron from Cleveland to Consett for use in the steelmaking process. (Beamish Museum)

closure of Consett steelworks in 1980, owing to various economic factors, meant there was no reason to continue operating the line up to Consett from the junction with the East Coast Main Line. His Royal Highness Prince Charles visited Consett by royal train, pulled by two Class 31 diesel locomotives, on a goodwill visit in December 1982, following the job losses owing to the closure of the steelworks. The end of the line was marked formally with a special railtour on 17 March 1984, hauled by Class 46 diesel locomotive 46026 *Leicestershire and Derbyshire Yeomanry*, fitted with a wreath, headboard and number plate from 9F Class locomotive 92099, which used to work the iron ore trains. The railtour ran from Newcastle Central along the line to the site of Consett station, long demolished by this

The 1834 S&TR lime and coal depot from West Boldon, as rebuilt at Beamish Museum.

History repeating itself. In late 2019, a training centre for the NEXUS Metro light rail system is under construction at South Shields on the site of the original workshops for the Stanhope & Tyne Railroad Company.

point. It had initially been planned to use a diesel multiple unit but had to be upgraded to a diesel locomotive with seven carriages after high demand for tickets. Calls were made, by the Derwentside Rail Action Group, to keep the line open and reinstate passenger services, but nothing came of it. As well as the rails being lifted, many bridges were demolished to improve the roads in the area.

Around the South Shields end of the line some small parts of the original route are still in use, and just to the south part of the line is used by freight services to and from Tyne Dock that come off the Brandling route at Brockley Whins. There is much irony in that this line, built in the 1830s to ship coal from the North East of England via the Tyne, has, until very recently, been used to import coal to the North East. Tyne Dock itself would be unrecognisable to T. E. Harrison. The dock itself has been filled in, with the 'dripping arches', immortalised in Catherine Cookson's novels, gone and huge warehouses taking the site of where coal staiths and their recipient vessels once were. Ships now moor at the quayside instead.

Most of the route of the line, using the deviations around Beamish and Annfield Plain, is open to pedestrians, cyclists and horse riders as part of the coast to coast cycle path. This starts at Sunderland and joins the route of the S&TR, near Victoria Viaduct, then, after crossing the A1, takes up the deviation route up to Consett, across Hownes Gill Viaduct, through Rowley and along the 1859 Burnhill deviation to reach Waskerley. It then travels across the moors, branching from the S&TR at Parkhead station where it continues via the Weatherhill and Rookhope trackbed. In some parts, the original S&TR trackbed not used for the cycle path or part of the modern railway network can still be clearly seen, but elsewhere it is obliterated by new developments. Those parts that do remain, together with surviving infrastructure, provide plenty of reminders of this remarkable railway.

Stonework remaining from the original Weatherhill incline engine house.

The north postal of Ifog Hill Tunnel, just seen in its steep-sided cutting, December 2019

Bibliography

Archival

Beamish Museum
Autobiography of George Hardy
Photographic Archive

Durham County Records Office
Records of Stockton & Darlington Railway
CP/Shl Records of Shildon locomotive works
D/Ki Records of Kitching Foundry
D/XD Records of Stockton & Darlington Railway

Head of Steam, Darlington Railway Museum Ken Hoole Study Centre
Ken Hoole Photographs & Documents collection
RH Inness notebooks

The National Archives
AN 13 British Transport Commission
RAIL 64 Brandling Junction Railway
RAIL 390 London & North Eastern Railway
RAIL 663 Stanhope & Tyne Railroad Company
RAIL 667 Stockton & Darlington Railway
RAIL 716 Wear & Derwent Junction Railway
RAIL 1021 TE Harrison

National Railway Museum
Records of Robert Stephenson & Co.

Published

Atkinson, F., *The Man Who Made Beamish: An Autobiography* (Gateshead: Northern Books, 1999).

Baldwin, J. H., 'The Stanhope and Tyne Railway: A Study in Business Failure' in *Early Railways: A Selection of Papers from the First International Railway Conference*, edited by Andy Guy and Jim Rees. (London: Newcomen Society, 2001) pp. 325–341.

Darsley, R., *Consett to South Shields via Beamish* (Midhurst: Middleton Press, 2009 (2016)).

Dawson, A., *Locomotives of the Victorian Railway: The Early Days of Steam* (Stroud: Amberley Publishing, 2019).

Donnelly, J., *South Pelaw Junction* http://www.southpelawjunction.co.uk

Hodgson, G. B., *The Borough of South Shields: From the Earliest Period to the Close of the Nineteenth Century* (Newcastle: Andrew Reid & Co., 1903).

Holmes, Dr P. J., *Stockton and Darlington Railway 1825–1975* (Ayr: First Avenue, 1975).

Hoole, K., *A Regional History of the Railways of Great Britain Volume 4: The North East* (Newton Abbot: David & Charles, 1965 (1978)).

Hoole, K., *North Eastern Locomotive Sheds* (Newton Abbot: David & Charles, 1972).

Mountford, C. E., *Rope & Chain Haulage: The Forgotten Element of Railway History* (Melton Mowbray: The Industrial Railway Society, 2013).

Pearce, T. R., *The Locomotives of the Stockton and Darlington Railway* (London: Historical Model Railway Society, 1996).

Proud, J. H., *The Chronicle of the Stockton & Darlington Railway to 1863* (North Eastern Railway Association, 2008) .

Rounthwaite, T. E., *The Railways of Weardale* (Railway Correspondence and Travel Society, 1965).

Tomlinson, W. W., *The North Eastern Railway: Its Rise and Development* (Newcastle: Andrew Reid, 1914).

Whishaw, F., *Railways of Great Britain and Ireland Practically Described and Illustrated* (London: John Weale, 1842).

Whittle, G., *The Railways of Consett and North-West Durham* (Newton Abbot: David & Charles, 1971).

Woods, N., *A Practical Treatise on Railroads* (London: Longman, Orme, Brown, Green, 1838).

Acknowledgements

As always, there are many more people than just the author involved in seeing a book through to completion. On a personal note, my thanks go to Romilly and Cocoa for both helping and tolerating me through the research, writing and editing process and aiding me where they can. Anthony Dawson, a fellow early railways writer, has been a great help, as has Julian Harrop at Beamish Museum in using their superb collections. The staff at Head of Steam – Darlington Railway Museum, National Railway Museum and The National Archives have all been very helpful. Various members of the North Eastern Railway Association have also pointed me in the right direction, Michael Ellison and Neil Mackay in particular. I would also like to say thanks to railway writers who have gone before me in writing about this railway, especially Frank Atkinson, Lionel Thomas Carswell 'Tom' Rolt, William Weaver Tomlinson and Neil Whittle. Thanks also go to Amberley Publishing for making this book a possibility. There are no doubt others I have missed, to whom I can only apologise.

STANHOPE AND TYNE RAIL-ROAD.

Detail from the cover of one of the S&TR's surviving sales ledgers. The train is unlike any known to have ran on the S&TR and shows a Stephenson-built 'Northumbrian' type locomotive, as used on the Liverpool & Manchester Railway.